House Beautiful

Your
Dream Bathroom

House Beautiful

Your
Dream Bathroom

Stylish Solutions for the Home

From the Editors of *House Beautiful*

HEARST BOOKS
A Division of Sterling Publishing Co., Inc.
NEW YORK

Produced by Spooky Cheetah Press, Stamford, CT
Edited by Brian Fitzgerald
Interior design by Kimberly Shake
Cover design by Margaret Rubiano

Library of Congress Cataloging-in-Publication Data Available.

10 9 8 7 6 5 4 3 2 1

Published by Hearst Books
A Division of Sterling Publishing Co., Inc.
387 Park Avenue South, New York, NY 10016

House Beautiful and Hearst Books are trademarks of Hearst Communications, Inc.

www.housebeautiful.com

For information about custom editions, special sales, premium and corporate purchases, please contact Sterling Special Sales Department at 800-805-5489 or specialsales@sterlingpub.com.

Distributed in Canada by Sterling Publishing
C/o Canadian Manda Group, 165 Dufferin Street
Toronto, Ontario, Canada M6K 3H6

Distributed in Australia by Capricorn Link (Australia) Pty. Ltd.
P.O. Box 704, Windsor, NSW 2756 Australia

Manufactured in China

Sterling ISBN 13: 978-1-58816-488-9
        ISBN 10: 1-58816-488-8

contents

Foreword   7

PART 1 design & style   9

Bathrooms by Design   11
planning ■ smart design ■ storage

Bathroom Styles   41
charming ■ contemporary ■ elegant
rustic ■ simple ■ spa ■ vintage

PART 2 details, details, details   79

Bathroom Cabinets   81
buying basics ■ finishing touches

Stunning Surfaces   91
countertops ■ walls ■ flooring

Fabulous Fixtures   117
sinks ■ faucets ■ showers ■ tubs ■ toilets

The Well-Lit Bath   155
natural light ■ artificial light

PART 3 making it happen   167

Working with Professionals   169
designers ■ architects ■ contractors ■ bids & contracts

Budgeting & Finance   185

Photography Credits   188

Index   190

foreword

In today's busy, wired world, everyone could use his or her own private getaway space, someplace pristine and tranquil to escape from the hustle and bustle. And there's no other room in the house that may be better suited for this escape than the bathroom.

Quiet, intimate, lined in cool tile and clear glass, the bathroom is more than a spot for a scented soak or a hot shower. Instead, think of the bath as a temple of daily renewal, a sanctuary devoted to you alone. And don't forget the practical perks: A sybaritic master bath is a great selling point if you ever put your house on the market, and you'll most likely recoup the cost of improvements on resale.

When it comes to design, remember that whether you prefer a luxurious space reminiscent of a grand hotel, one with a meditative, Zen-like aesthetic or a cheery, light-filled room that appeals to your whimsical side, conveying your personal style begins with the materials you choose. To get you started, we've put together some of our favorite ideas on surfaces, storage, fixtures and fittings. So go ahead—make a splash in your bath!

DESIGN & STYLE

◀ A concrete tub surround lends a serene effect to this bath.

bathrooms by design

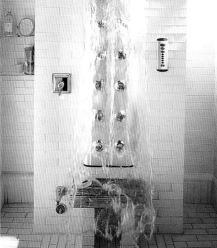

▲ With its 10 jets, this Body Spa system combines whirlpool action with hydro-massage in a relaxing waterfall shower.

Serene or splashy, the bathroom should be a retreat that reflects your style and your lifestyle. But planning this all-important space can get a little slippery. Start by considering what you really want from your new bath. Are you hoping to improve the aesthetics of an out-of-date design, introduce some of the newest amenities or completely rework an awkward layout? Are you fulfilling a long-time dream of a luxurious master bath or do you mainly wish to increase the resale value of your home?

Determining the scope of the project, as well as the purpose of the remodel, will guide you in developing a budget for the job. If you plan to live in the house for some time or if you're building a new home, you may decide to go all out. But if you are remodeling for eventual resale, beware of over-improving: Try to get a sense of what other homes in your area feature to avoid investing more than the market will bear. Keep your improvements to visible changes that will help your house "show" well—new flooring or countertops, for example.

It's impossible to design an effective bath—or any room, for that matter—without taking the time to evaluate your personal priorities. More room? More light? More luxury? Think carefully about your likes and dislikes, and then start dreaming!

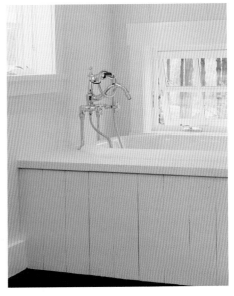

▼ An elaborate tub filler adds a nice contrast to the simplicity of this oversize soaking tub.

▲ This vintage bath gets a new lease on life from the splash of color that's echoed on the walls, the tub, the shower curtain and within the pattern of the floor tiles.

You don't have to look far to see that the bathroom has evolved from a simple space for bathing and grooming to a luxurious getaway. Still, the bathroom is a utilitarian space, and you must start any remodel with practical considerations, such as layout, longevity and low maintenance. For example, you'll want to select counter-tops that are easy to maintain and won't show nicks, scratches or stains, and cabinets that have an easy-to-clean, long-wearing finish.

The most important first step in planning your new bathroom is to set a budget and then divide it into two parts: labor and materials. You don't want to overspend in one area and leave yourself short for the other. Then start comparison shopping. Visit at least two or three home centers or showrooms before you purchase any fixtures or furnishings. You'll have a better understanding of the styles available, as well as the different companies that manufacture bathroom products.

You should also try to get a feel for the level of service that each company offers. You want to look for products from reputable companies that will be able to offer parts and service later.

The best way to start planning your bathroom update is to mentally divide the space into three zones: bath and shower; sink and grooming; and toilet and bidet. Think carefully about what each area should comprise, then consider the basic space and planning requirements.

Finding Your Style

Confused about your style? Consider these design professionals' tips for determining what will work for you.

• Look through magazines, books, bathroom showrooms, even other people's homes to mine for ideas. Keep a three-ring binder with pictures of what you like—anything from individual fixtures to entire rooms. Also include pouches to hold material samples, such as paint chips and wallpaper samples.

• Review your style file every so often and get rid of inconsistent ideas and anything that no longer fits your tastes or needs. Narrow down your choices by getting a second opinion from professionals and friends. If you can't decide between two or more items, make price the deciding factor.

• The design of your bathroom should reflect the personality of your family, so make sure you're following your heart—not just current trends.

▲ Porcelain tile in a matte finish mimics weathered sandstone for a rustic look.

▲ If you want your new master bath to be a showpiece, you'll need a scene-stealing tub.

Bath/Shower Area

In a sense, this area is the focal point of the room, so it deserves special attention. You'll need to consider the actual shower or bathtub and also the surrounding elements to ensure that getting in and out of the bathing area is safe and comfortable.

Here's one place you may want to splurge, creating an at-home spa environment. Note, however, that while many homeowners list a whirlpool tub as their most coveted bathroom feature, most people actually prefer showers. So you might want to consider indulging in a luxurious steam shower unit before you decide on a fancy tub.

To determine your wants and needs, you have to consider a few things. What fixtures do you want? Do you prefer a separate shower and tub or a single tub/shower unit? What about oversize models, like a steam shower or a whirlpool tub for two?

Space is a major consideration. The inside of a typical shower enclosure is 32 by 32 inches, but most people need at least 38 by 38 inches to shampoo their hair easily. You must also plan for proper clearance around shower and tub areas. A minimum of 21 inches between the tub/shower and a wall or other obstacle must be maintained so you can easily walk past the fixture;

but 30 inches is more comfortable. If two or more people share the bath, a 42- to 60-inch space is required to ensure that they can pass by each other without colliding.

Have you considered tub safety? When planning a tub area, think about how you—and your kids—will get in and out of it. Sunken tubs and those with steps leading to a high platform are not considered safe; a low platform, however, is ideal, since you can sit on the edge and swing your legs into the tub easily. Faucets should be within reach from outside the tub, so you won't have to climb in and out to turn the water on and off.

▼ The right accessories—like an old-fashioned tub filler—can lend a touch of Old World style to even the most up-to-date whirlpool tub.

▲ The brilliant marine blue walls in this bathroom make the white wainscot appear even crisper.

▲ Each accessory—from faucets to window handles—adds a timeless appeal to this bathroom.

STYLE NOTES

Penny Wise . . .

Most bathroom planners advise homeowners to buy the best quality they can afford when it comes to plumbing fixtures. A $50 showerhead and a $300 showerhead may both do the trick, but the pricier one features inner workings made of durable bronze. The less expensive fixture is made primarily with plastic parts.

▲ Rich beige tones and stylish wallcoverings create an understated sanctuary in this bath.

▲ Laminate cabinets and solid-surface countertops are easy to maintain.

Sink/Grooming Area

The sink and grooming area of the bathroom must fulfill a number of requirements. Since you may often be in a hurry here—dashing to work or primping for a night out—you'll want to plan for maximum efficiency. The space should also be easy to maintain, so consider surfacing and sink materials that wipe clean with minimal effort. And aesthetics are key: faucets, countertops, sinks, mirrors, lighting and cabinetry are all important elements in achieving the look you want. The most important factors to consider here are features and space requirements.

If two people use the space, you may want double sinks and extra cabinetry to keep the morning rush as organized as possible. Do you prefer pedestal sinks or vanities? Pedestal fixtures have an elegant appeal, but vanities offer more storage. Would you like a fixed mirror above the sink or medicine cabinets that open?

You'll also need room to maneuver. In general you'll need 21 to 30 inches of space between the sink and a wall or fixture opposite, and 42 inches to towel off. A minimum of 2 to 6 inches is the standard distance from the sink edge to the adjacent wall. Expand that

to 12 to 18 inches if you install cabinetry below the counter. Double sinks usually require 5 to 8 feet of counter.

Toilet/Bidet Area

Often overlooked in favor of more exciting bath zones, the toilet and bidet area is extremely important to the overall comfort of the room. Take the following into account as you plan this area of your bath: What features do you want? Would you like a compartmentalized toilet area? If so, do you want a window in this area? Do you want a one- or two-piece toilet? One-piece units are easier to clean, but more

▲ Surfacing can make or break a beautiful bath. Here creamy concrete tops a vanity area for a look that is at once modern and elegant.

Room to Grow

If you're one of the lucky few homeowners who has an extra bathroom just for the children, you'll want to create a space that grows with them. The whimsical setup at right includes stylish fixtures especially developed for young children learning to use adult devices. The highlight of this bathroom is the remote-control Zoë toilet, which adds functional fun to potty training with a bidet-like washlet, a seat warmer and a disk fan. Also featured in this room is a pedestal sink with a safely anchored Lucite step stool that allows youngsters to easily reach the basin.

expensive. Do you want a bidet? Do you even have enough space for this extra fixture? You'll need to plan at least 30 inches from left to right just for the toilet. If it is in a separate compartment, increase that to 36 inches. You'll want to leave a minimum of 21 inches of floor space in front of the toilet, though 30 inches is even better. If a door opens into the bathroom from a wall alongside the toilet, make sure there is at least 16 inches of knee space from the casing of the door to the front of the fixture. If you'll be including a bidet, allow at least 30 inches of space to separate it from the toilet.

▲ Separate his-and-her sinks make the morning rush more manageable.

▲ The subtle design of this bidet and skirted toilet works with many decorating styles.

Making It Fit

Dreaming about a luxurious master bath and actually having the space to include all the amenities you desire are two different things. It's easy to fit an imaginary space with two vanities, a steam shower, an exercise area and the like, but it's significantly more difficult to squeeze these features into your real-life bathroom, which is probably quite a bit smaller than the one that floats in your fantasies.

If you're building a new house, of course, you'll have somewhat more flexibility. But take the time to make sure the blueprints allow enough space for everything you want to include in the bath—if they don't, ask your architect to alter the plans. And be realistic: Before the project begins, decide which features you really want and need and which you may never use.

Once you've decided what amenities your new bath must include, you may have to get creative in finding the space to make your dream a reality. One common option is to bump out an exterior wall to garner extra square footage. But beware of the expenses involved. Adding square footage to a new house will raise the base cost, so you may have to re-evaluate your con-

struction budget before giving the go-ahead. And tearing out and replacing existing exterior walls in an older home can get complicated. You'll have to find materials to match the exterior siding and trim, and make the addition blend with the architectural style of the house. If you decide to go this route, plan for the addition before construction or renovation begins—changes made partway through the project are much more expensive.

If you'd prefer not to change the exterior of your home, you'll need to focus on the interior, finding unused space to help expand your bath. One

▼ The separate toilet compartment is taken to a new level of luxury in this bathroom.

▲ This corner bath tucks into a nook, so even the smallest bathroom can include a soaking tub.

▲ A rich wood floor adds warmth to the bath—just make sure it's properly sealed.

▲ This compact vanity brings simple beauty to the bath, and it can fit almost anywhere.

▶ Not just another bathroom fixture, this freestanding tub resembles a work of art.

good option is to take space from the master bedroom and use it for a larger, adjoining master bath. An extra closet that backs up to the bath is prime real estate as well. If you'll miss the storage space, see if you can devote a wall of the master bedroom to a row of closets. If neither of these options is available to you, you'll have to look a bit farther afield. Consider taking part of the attic, a utility room, empty space under the eaves, or even a balcony and adding it to the square footage of your bath. These spaces might seem a bit more challenging to work with, but a good architect or designer can help with the transformation.

Finally, if you're stuck with the space as it is—and you can find absolutely no way to expand it—make the most of every square inch. Think carefully about how you'll use the space and divide it into activity zones: bathing, grooming, etc. Make a list of every item you use while in the bath. Then outfit cabinetry with storage features tailored to your lifestyle. Reducing clutter will make a small bath seem more expansive. If there's room, include a linen closet, taking advantage of accessories like roll-out hampers and divided drawers to keep laundry and toiletries organized and out of the way. Also consider installing shallow

shelves or cabinets in the space between wall studs—this can maximize storage in a compact space as well.

If you're like most homeowners considering a remodeling or new construction project, you probably have plenty of dreams about your new bath and no idea how to implement them. You know you want an old-fashioned claw-foot tub, a separate toilet compartment or a steam shower built for two in the bath, but you can't quite picture them as a reality. Don't worry, your architect, builder or designer can. But before you start to consult with an expert, just be sure you can express exactly what you want.

▼ This combination shower and whirlpool offers the best of both bathing options.

▲ This sink combines old-fashioned charm with contemporary convenience.

A Sensation of Space

Create the illusion of more space in your bath by choosing materials and lighting that draw the eye up and visually add height to the room.

• Light-colored materials make any space feel bigger. You can make a small shower stall feel larger by selecting white tile and taking it up to the ceiling, rather than stopping at the top of the door. Add a light and a recessed wall niche for toiletries, and suddenly the room feels more open.

• Use half-walls to separate task areas—rather than full walls that tend to break up the space and cut off light. If your budget allows, consider bumping out one wall to add a window seat.

• You don't need to be a magician to use mirrors effectively—nor is this technique something new. Installing a mirror is one of the oldest and easiest design tricks used to make a room appear larger. However, it's important to carefully consider the placement of the mirror.

▲ This basin features a narrow rim and a unique oval shape.

▲ A hand-painted above-counter basin like this one will brighten any room.

▲ Subtle tone variations among the wall tiles adds interest to a monochromatic room.

Sketch It Out

Getting your project out of your head and onto paper is one of the best ways to clarify your goals—both for yourself and for any professionals you hire. To help you take this first step, we've included some tools on the following page that will help you make your own preliminary blueprint—you just need to supply the graph paper. Start by photocopying the page of templates, then cut out the ones you need.

Next, measure your space carefully, including window and door openings, projecting radiators and the like. Letting each segment of the grid equal six inches, draw your bath onto the graph paper using the measurements you've just taken. Now comes the fun part—placing the templates on the grid and setting up your room.

You may find that all the elements you'd hoped to include just won't fit. Don't worry: A skilled architect or certified bath designer can often "find" space you didn't know you had. After all, this is just a preliminary plan to help you develop an actual design with your team of professionals.

Careful planning can maximize efficiency and style in even the smallest space. Make a point of visiting nearby showrooms for product ideas and ways to maximize your choices. Determine whether you will have enough room for desired amenities, such as a second sink, a whirlpool, a shower separate from the tub or a separate toilet compartment. Make sure that the shower door or any cabinet doors won't interrupt circulation when open. If the bathroom is intended for a couple or for several family members to share, two people should be able to comfortably occupy the room at the same time.

Once you have a sense of what your space will accommodate, it's time to start the all-important planning stage.

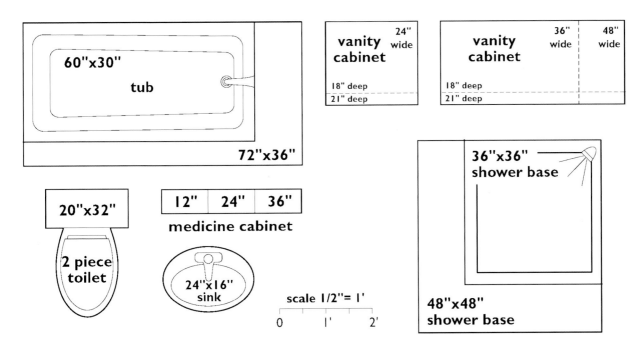

60"x30" tub		
72"x36"		

vanity cabinet — 24" wide
18" deep
21" deep

vanity cabinet — 36" wide / 48" wide
18" deep
21" deep

20"x32"			

12" | 24" | 36"
medicine cabinet

2 piece toilet

24"x16" sink

scale 1/2"= 1'
0   1'   2'

36"x36" shower base

48"x48" shower base

▲ These small-scale drawings of the essential elements will help you create the best plan for your new bathroom.

▼ Sleek handles accentuate this double vanity's high-tech persona.

▲ Luxurious extras, like this oversize showerhead, can turn the master bath into a true haven.

Nine-tenths of a successful remodeling or building project is careful consideration of all the elements involved before work even begins. Think long and hard about what you want from the project, what work will be involved, how much you can spend and how much time you can devote to the job. New ideas will be very expensive to implement once the work has begun, so make all your decisions early on. Don't forget to think about the future: If you'll be improving other areas of your house or adding on down the road, take care not to reposition plumbing or structural elements in spots that will obstruct future work.

Remember the Bottom Line

Our remodeling fantasies and the funds needed to execute them are often not in line. To avoid disappointment—and to ensure a successful project—it is essential that you develop a realistic budget early on. Start by getting some rough estimates for design and construction fees for a project of your size. Next, shop around for prices on the types of materials you'd like to include. Add about 20 percent for a contingency "slush fund" and then compare this number to your available assets. Trim or slash as necessary to come up with your project budget, then stick to it. As you choose professionals, make

sure they understand and respect your budget. It will be their job to make the most of every penny.

To avoid stress, set a realistic time frame for the job. Bad weather, labor and materials shortages and a host of other unforeseen challenges can delay a remodeling or construction project, so be sure to allow plenty of time for the job. Ask your contractor for an estimate of the length of the project, then factor in extra weeks or months depending on its scope. Never try to meet a "deadline"—a new bath before your mother-in-law moves in, for instance—you'll only end up sacrificing quality for speed.

▼ Glass block can provide a measure of privacy while keeping the room open and bright.

▲ This étagère uses empty wall space to house towels and toiletries.

▲ A rubbed bronze finish on this faucet is the perfect counterpoint to the surrounding stone.

STYLE NOTES

Taking Measure

When you sketch a preliminary design for your bath, plan for adequate elbow room. The National Kitchen & Bath Association (NKBA) offers the following guidelines (available online at www.nkba.com):

• Doorways should be at least 32 inches wide.

• A shower or tub with a showerhead should have a minimum floor-to-ceiling height of 80 inches.

• The clear floor space from the front edge of all fixtures (sink, toilet, bidet, tub and shower) to any opposite bath fixture, wall or obstacle should be at least 30 inches.

• Keep at least 18 inches of space between the centerline of the toilet and/or bidet and any bath fixture, wall or other obstacle.

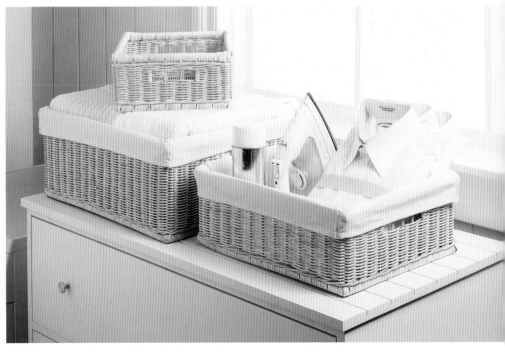

▲ Different-size baskets offer a handy—and inexpensive—storage option.

▲ This beautiful sink has a subtle hue that provides color without overwhelming the rest of the room's design scheme.

▲ To make a small room appear larger, use wallpaper that features a small print, choosing colors in soft hues like peach or green.

Color Your World

When advising their clients on how to select color for a room, most interior designers offer the same piece of wisdom: Regardless of how trendy a color may be, if it doesn't please you, it's not the right choice.

The most important thing is to select a hue that meets your needs. Want to warm things up? Try sun-drenched paint in toasty shades of red, orange or yellow. For a more tranquil space, use a fresh, calming coat of green, blue or lavender. Good colors to consider for a spalike bath are those that gravitate toward gentle hues evocative of earth and water. Subtle blues and greens and warm sand tones soothe the eye and calm the spirit.

There are endless possibilities for color and finishes to use in any room. However, keep in mind a few things when picking them. Take into consideration the natural and artificial light of the room and observe it at different times during the day. If you've selected bold colors, consider using two shades lighter than your original choice. When painted on a large surface any color becomes more intense. Keep in mind that a bathroom is essentially a working room and a lighter color, such as yellow, pale blue or off-white, will help reflect more light. Unless you're deco-

rating a small guest bathroom where you could dabble in some wild colors, it is probably wiser to choose more neutral shades.

Choosing the Right Palette

Once you've selected a base color, the fun really begins. The ultimate combination of colors plays an important role in determining the tone of a room. For instance, cool colors (blues, greens and purples) have been proven to be calming, while hot colors (reds, oranges and yellows) exhilarate. Less obvious, however, is the fact that the ways in which colors are combined will also influence the tenor of a space. And

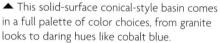

▲ This solid-surface conical-style basin comes in a full palette of color choices, from granite looks to daring hues like cobalt blue.

▲ For a bit of modern splash, consider designing your own mosaic artwork for the bathroom walls. Here the variety of tile sizes and colors creates a dazzling backdrop for bathing.

the choice of combinations is vast. For example, a designer may choose to augment the base color with varying values (lightness and darkness) or intensities (brightness and dullness) of the same one. Or he or she may opt to incorporate entirely new colors. Designers often look to the color wheel—a tool used by visual artists that illustrates how colors relate to one another—when making these decisions. Some combinations are comforting, others more energizing. When determining your own color scheme, experiment before settling on a final choice. And above all, be confident to go with the one that feels right to you.

▲ Don't be afraid to be bold! Together, the rich wall color and black-and-white floor tiles used in this bathroom lend an air of sophistication.

▲ This tri-panel shower door has three equally sized sections that run along a bottom-track system—a design that gives bathers an entry that's 32 percent larger than that of a typical tub.

First developed to help the elderly and people with disabilities, universal design often came with a stigma. People thought that employing the principles of universal design meant that you had to have an institutional look of a hospital. Today, though, this is not the case: By making simple adjustments, you can not only devise a plan that will make the space more comfortable for users of any size, age and ability, but you will also add value to your home at resale.

Getting Started

To implement a universal design in your bath, you'll first need to examine your bathroom space—the actual size of the room and the activity zones needed, as well as the features and materials that you'll use in it. For example, baths designed using the principles of universal design are often larger than the standard 5-by-7-foot space typical of many homes. They should be large enough to accommodate two people at the same time and to include a separate toilet compartment for privacy. This way, parents can help children bathe and change clothing, or a caregiver can assist a disabled member of the family.

In the bathing area, take care to choose the right tub, shower and accessories and to position each of them appropriately. Opt for a custom-built shower that has no threshold, so a wheelchair user can roll right in. (Some prefabricated units also offer this design.) Plan to install a seat inside the

▼ This ADA-compliant shower unit includes factory-installed grab bars and a plastic seat for maximum ease and comfort. The floor is pebbled for improved traction.

▲ In this bathroom a wheelchair-height transfer seat at the head of the bathtub promotes easy access. A deck-mounted handshower is conveniently located nearby.

▲ So much more than a pretty face, this ADA-compliant vanity allows wheelchair users to roll right up to the sink.

shower, and make sure that shower-heads are mounted on adjustable rods, so the fixture can slide up and down for users of any height. It's also crucial to install grab bars inside the shower. These bars should support more than 250 pounds, so they must be installed in the wall studs. No longer institutional in appearance, today's grab bars are decorative enough to be used as towel bars elsewhere in the bath (but actual towel bars should never be used in place of grab bars).

The safest bathtub is one built into a platform—that way, an elderly or disabled user can sit on the edge and swing his or her legs into the tub. But there are also some common situations where getting in and out of the bath may pose a challenge—for someone recovering from an injury or bathing a baby, for instance. Whatever the situation, an extra-large deck or "transfer space" at the head of the tub that acts as a built-in seat for easing in and out of the water can make these maneuvers much easier. If you plan to include this feature, make sure it extends at least 15 inches beyond the tub.

Faucets and controls should be placed on the entry side of the tub so that someone outside the tub can turn the water on and off. A handheld spray shower will make shampooing—and cleaning the bathtub—a lot easier.

As for the rest of the bath: The bath platform and all flooring throughout the bath should be slip resistant. In baths with two sinks, it makes sense to vary counter heights to accommodate users of different heights. You might install one sink at 36 inches in a vanity with drawers and cabinets for storage,

◀ The traditional appearance of this tub/shower set belies its up-to-date capabilities, which include a built-in thermostat that can be preset to prevent scalding.

STYLE NOTES

Safety at a Glance

The following guidelines will make your spaces accessible to the very young and the very old.

• Lay nonslip floors.

• Lower light switches to 44 inches from the floor to afford access to a seated person or a child.

• For wheelchair accessibility, allow for a 32-inch-wide doorway, a 31-inch-high sink with knee space below and a shower entrance that has a flat threshold and is wide enough for a wheelchair.

• Install a height-adjustable showerhead that the user can easily adapt to a handheld sprayer.

• Install grab bars able to support at least 250 pounds around the tub, toilet and in the shower.

• Add a pull-down or fixed seat in the shower or tub.

• Install easy-to-manipulate single-handle faucets for the sinks, shower and tub.

• Make sure all faucets feature scald protection.

and install the second at 30 inches, leaving the space underneath open. This allows someone to use the sink from a seated position, and it also leaves room for a small set of steps for a young child to use. Pedestal or wall-hung sinks are a good choice for a small bath—just be sure to include extra storage on either side. All faucets should have lever handles, which are easier to manipulate, and should be equipped with temperature-limit stops to prevent scalding.

Including all or some of these features will make your bath a comfortable haven for everyone who uses it and can be a selling point in years to come.

▲ Universal design can be beautiful and still meet ADA standards. This bathroom features an adjustable-height countertop and ample use of safety bars.

▲ This toilet model is two inches taller than standard toilets (the same height as a household chair), making it easier for the elderly to use.

▲ Whether you're nursing an injury or trying to hold onto a soapy child, a single-handle lever-type faucet is easier to use.

▲ This sink-and-countertop unit combines contemporary styling and smart design for a beautiful fixture that can accommodate wheelchair users.

▲ This whirlpool tub makes maintenance a snap by eliminating the pipes and channels where debris usually accumulates.

◀ Clean and crisp cabinetry is a great choice for bathrooms of any architectural era. Paired with contemporary elements like mosaic tiles and a vessel sink, the cabinets take on a modern look; more traditional design elements would lend a classic twist.

Going High Tech

Whether you're building a new bath or remodeling an existing one, you should check out the high-tech products making a splash on the residential scene. Thanks to new technology, amenities that were once exclusive to hotels and spas are now available for the home. Of course, the more luxurious the item, the higher the price tag. But with everything from shower radios to combination whirlpool/entertainment centers available, there's something for everyone.

Getting Energy Efficient

Some of the smartest energy-saving solutions can be found in the bath—ideas that can save up to 30 percent or more on your energy bill. One way to curb energy waste and let the savings flow is to go low flow. An average family can reduce water usage by 17,000 gallons a year simply by replacing old showerheads and faucets with high-efficiency low-flow showerheads and faucet aerators. Older showerheads can use up to 6 gallons of water per

minute (gpm), while newer heads spray out 2.5 gpm or less. Low-flush toilets can stop the flood as well, using a maximum of 1.6 gallons per flush (gpf) compared to the 3.5 to 5 gpf used by older models.

When counting up energy savings, you should also consider the hot water used for showers and faucets. Put your electric water heater on the clock and install an automatic timer that turns the heater off at night and back on again in the morning. Better yet, add a

▲ This splash-proof CD-MP3 player offers sensational sound and includes a shower hook and push-button controls specially designed for soapy fingers.

▲ This soothing vertical shower spa gives you the ultimate shower experience—choose from body sprays and a multifunction showerhead and handshower.

▲ This whirlpool tub includes a home theater featuring a 42-inch high-definition plasma monitor, surround sound and a DVD/CD/AM/FM stereo system.

▶ Turn every day into a spa experience with heated towel bars, available in either wall- or floor-mounted models.

solar-boosting hot water unit and take advantage of the sun's rays. On a sunny day, you can soak in a savings of up to 90 percent off your heating bill. Wrap existing water heaters with an insulating blanket and you can reduce heat loss by more than 25 percent. Depending on where your water heater is located (inside or outside), you may not need an insulating jacket on newer models that are well insulated. How can you tell? If your heater is warm to the touch, then wrap it up.

▲ With freestanding cabinets like these, your bathroom design options are virtually limitless.

Feeling the squeeze in your small bath? You're not alone. Increasing storage space is often a top priority for homeowners remodeling an existing bath. The real trick to good bath design is finding ways to carve out more storage in your existing space, so it pays to turn to a pro.

If you can't add on to your bathroom, your best bet is to make the most of what you have. For example, if your bathroom includes a double sink, but only one person washes up at a time, consider going with a single bowl and using the extra space for storage. Instead of having two sinks in a 72-inch vanity, you can center one in the middle and add accessible, above-counter storage on either side to create two grooming areas.

Another area people often overlook is the space above the toilet. By installing a wall cabinet here, you can really take advantage of unused real estate. You can also use your medicine cabinet to optimize storage space.

Cabinet styles range from single-door units to those that span the entire width of the wall. If you have the wall space above your sink, a larger medicine cabinet is a great way to make the most of it. You can also use hooks and racks to great effect—some thick towels or fluffy robes hung behind the bathroom door are practical and also lend the room a spalike feel. And don't forget to keep some cleaning supplies under the sink. A clean and shiny bathroom will make the space look bigger.

▼ This frameless medicine cabinet offers high-end features like all-steel construction, external and interior mirrors and a choice of heights and depths—all at a moderate price.

▲ This vanity provides ample storage, and the cabinets (tall and small) are easy to move around for perfect placement of one or more pieces.

STYLE NOTES

On the Hook

Wall hooks are a natural for towels, robes and nightgowns. You can place them next to tubs and showers or on the backs of doors. Shaker-style peg racks are another great option for hanging nightgowns and bathrobes.

▲ When is a shelf more than a shelf? When its architectural detailing sets it apart, a shelf can become a focal point, too.

Time to Get Organized

With today's hectic schedules, anything that helps you save a minute or two in the morning is appreciated. That's where increased storage and efficiency come into play in the bathroom—the more organized you can be in the morning, the faster you can get on with your day. Here are some ways to keep clutter to a minimum in the bathroom, so you can find what you need instantly.

Consider installing:

• Pull-out drawer trays in cabinets so you can store and reach items even in the back of the vanity.

• A medicine cabinet instead of a simple mirror. Medicine cabinets with several shelves of storage space are more attractive than ever and can be recessed so that they don't stick out into the room the way they used to.

• Racks or metal baskets on cabinet doors to hold small appliances, such as hair dryers and curling irons—and their pesky cords.

• Cubbies and open shelves in odd corners, not unlike narrow cabinets for trays sometimes found in kitchens.

• A shelf around the perimeter of your bathroom or on one long wall, about a foot below the ceiling. This can hold decorative knickknacks to get them off countertops.

▲ No longer just metal boxes stuck haphazardly to the wall, today's medicine cabinets have gone all out for luxury and convenience.

◀ With tapered legs and classically styled glass door inserts, this freestanding cabinet creates the perfect centerpiece for any bath.

▲ Small enough to fit in the corner of a bathroom, yet large enough to hold towels and accessories, this three-tier table is at home in a variety of decors.

▲ This countertop cabinet makes great use of the extra space between twin sinks and offers a smart combination of open shelves and small drawers.

▲ Perfect for today's "unfitted" bathrooms, individual furniture pieces can offer all the practical storage of built-in cabinetry with a more personal effect.

▲ This shower curtain (or liner) covered with mesh pockets provides space for shampoo, razors, even your rubber ducky! And installation is a snap.

Get Cubed

Wouldn't it be great if your furniture changed along with your needs? That's the concept behind the inexpensive modular furniture system called Q-Bits. With seven cube, shelf and feet components, Q-Bits is almost like playing with blocks. The pieces can be configured into everything from towel storage to an auxiliary medicine cabinet. Use the cube with a door for hiding away toiletries, the open cube for storing towels and the cube with drawers for stowing beauty supplies.

▲ A platform that surrounds the tub offers a beautiful storage solution for towels, bath products, even flowers.

▶ This tall, glass-front cabinet provides plenty of storage for towels and shampoos.

BATHROOM STYLES

Charming

Contemporary

Elegant

Rustic

Simple

Spa

Vintage

◀ This bathroom gets an airy feeling from an oversize mirror that reflects sunlight from the window and glossy black surfaces.

bathroom styles

▲ Crafted of maple with a natural finish, this custom cabinetry offers sleek lines that are uninterrupted by hardware, lending a contemporary air to any bath.

Today's baths have morphed from grooming spaces to personal sanctuaries. And whether your taste is contemporary, vintage or spa, there are ideas and resources to render each vision a reality.

Settling on a style is the first thing you need to determine when planning any remodeling or building project, and it can be the easiest or most difficult part of the job. Some homeowners have a look in mind from the get-go, while others take longer to choose, vacillating between country charm or city chic, plush luxe or simple elegance. If you're still on the fence, here's a good jumping-off point: How do you want your new bath to make you feel?

Energized? Relaxed? Reassured? Once you know the effect you want, think about the colors and textures that will best create that effect. Materials, from fabrics to flooring, should reinforce the mood set by the color palette. Sheer fabrics and pale, reflective surfaces are a natural for a soothing look. Rich, nubby materials like velvet and chenille and textural surfacing like limestone or slate have a cozier look. Bright colors, strong patterns and shinier finishes can create an effect of vibrant energy. As you're shopping, keep in mind that the bath is not a room that you want to renovate regularly. Shop around and make sure your choices are those you will be happy with for years to come.

charming

In situations where privacy isn't a major consideration, sheer curtains impart more light than heavyweight fabrics and dry faster when splashes occur. In tune with this room's cheerful disposition, these diaphanous curtains frame a spectacular vista of treetops and bright, sunny sky.

Everyone has his or her own idea of what charming means—though many would be hard pressed to put it into words. Whimsical, airy designs that hearken back to simpler times, romantic touches that bring a smile to our faces, sunlit spaces that warm our hearts—all of these things lend charm to any room. Smaller, cozier rooms are also more apt to be called charming than vast, open spaces.

If you think this is the right look for you, there are several ways you can bring this delightful sense of comfort and charm to your bath.

Pale hues and pristine white are great choices for creating an idyllic escape. These crisp colors bring a sense of freshness to the space and help open it up. Adding custom moldings and beadboard call to mind turn-of-the-century cottages and beach houses—for an extra touch of whimsy, add white tiles painted with delicate flowers. Mullioned windows flanked by delicate curtains help complete the picture.

Out-of-the-ordinary storage solutions, like an antique table for toiletries or a cupboard for linens and supplies, also lend a touch of charm to the bath. Choosing a weathered finish coupled with nickel-plated fixtures for the pieces lends understated personality. And don't forget that it's your personal touches that add the most charm to any room. A quaint room is the perfect place to display crockery pots filled with wildflowers, jars of scented soap or a bowlful of beach glass.

▲ According to experts, green is an easy color on the eye. Evocative of harmony and nature, it can also pack a wallop in its acidic, citrusy shades.

▲ Elevating the room from utilitarian to elegant, hand-painted tiles accent the tub surround and the shower, interjecting color without overpowering the scene.

▲ Personal touches—like the antique brush and hand mirror, coupled with a glass perfume tray—add old-fashioned appeal to this grooming area.

▲ Tiles that echo hues found in nature lend a soothing touch to this bath.

▲ A clear glass shower enclosure keeps the room feeling more open. A flap at the top of the door can be closed when the shower is utilizing steam and opened for everyday use.

Buck the Trends

To help select features that you'll like over time, don't spend a lot on trendy designs. Shop around without thinking about price. Pick out what you like, but don't buy anything. If by the following week, you haven't thought about your selections, they probably weren't right for you. If, on the other hand, the products you selected have taken up residence in your daydreams, you'll probably enjoy them for years to come.

◀ Crisp white beadboard and built-in glass shelves add to this bath's sunny appeal.

▲ The original tub in this bathroom was treated to a new marble surround. With wide muntins and moldings, the windows add a touch of romance.

◀ Period-style light fixtures illuminate the vanity area. The brushed-nickel sconces are part of a lighting scheme that includes recessed spots overhead and a special fixture to brighten the shower.

▲ An antique beveled mirror in a white frame enhances the soothing mood of this bathroom.

▼ Traditional elements like painted wood accents and marble surfaces are paired with clean lines and a strong wall color for a one-of-a-kind look.

Creative Solutions

Imaginative touches will yield pretty, practical results for a charming bath.

• Add architectural wonders. More than just decorative additions, moldings help offset windows and doors and interject an instant sense of history to the room.

• Get white hot. Nothing draws attention or affords a better contrast than glossy white paint. Durable and fresh, this paint is a perfect choice for a hardworking room.

• Look for furniture finds. Antique or flea market surprises—cupboards, chairs, stools—are serviceable and packed with personality. Consider recruiting an old dresser as a vanity or enlisting a stool as a seat or table.

▲ A soothing color scheme of off-white, gray and taupe—mixed with plenty of sunlight—creates a welcoming ambiance in this master bath.

▲ This bathroom gets classic detailing from semicustom cabinetry, including an oversize medicine cabinet designed to replicate the look of an antique wardrobe.

▲ With its vast expanses of dark woods, gleaming surfaces and angled lines, this bathroom embodies the contemporary feel.

Streamlined, organized, crisp and clean—a contemporary design eschews fussy touches in favor of sleek lines and gleaming surfaces. This style of design is just perfect for smaller spaces since it often relies on a combination of natural materials, such as wood, metal, stone and glass, for a feeling of openness and light.

But achieving the right look with a contemporary design can be tricky. Strong lines and simple forms can only go so far: Too much glass and metal,

and too little personality, can create a space that's cold and uncomfortable. But when contemporary is done right, there's nothing as exciting. Though the look is definitely cutting edge, there's nothing stark or forbidding about it— on the contrary, the light-filled bath feels warm and inviting. And this design doesn't have to be all or nothing. There are varying degrees to a contemporary bath. You can—and should—tailor your design to suit your style and personality.

As with most design schemes, the right results can be achieved with a feel—and an eye—for the right materials and design elements. Naturally textured elements like slate floor tiles and mosaic tiles provide a welcome contrast to smooth wall tiles and a wide expanse of mirror above the sinks. Playful lines—adding a curve to the silhouette of the tub or shower, for instance—inject a sense of humor and soften the look of the room without dominating the design.

▲ The vanity cabinets in this bath may have sleek lines and bright red accents (applied with an aniline dye), but the warmth of the wood shines through.

▲ It appears to be straight out of the 1920s, but despite the art deco styling, this cabinet is strictly twenty-first century. A mirrored interior and adjustable shelves make it an eye-catching and practical addition to any bath.

▲ A wide mirror is set over twin sinks in a matte marble counter in this contemporary bath. A concealed medicine cabinet keeps toiletries stowed away without cluttering the space.

▲ This contemporary faucet can be mounted on the wall or the washbasin and can be turned to meet the needs of right- or left-handed people.

▲ The pared-down look of this wall-mounted sink combined with warm beige walls and floor tiles helps create a relaxing atmosphere.

STYLE NOTES

Keep It Clean

Contemporary bathrooms often feature a lot of gleaming surfaces—such as faucets, countertops, light fixtures and knobs. Keeping a bathroom like this sparkling is a key to making the room seem bigger and cleaner. A handy tip for staying on top of this chore: Before tossing any washcloth or hand towel in the hamper, use it to wipe around the sink and shine anything glass or chrome. You can also keep the space spick-and-span by setting aside an area where you will store bathroom cleaning supplies. The easier it is for you to access these items, the more inclined you will be to use them.

◀ Gleaming black quartz surfaces create an edgy counterpoint to the warm wood cabinetry and sunny yellow walls in this bath.

▲ An oval ceramic countertop washbasin adds sophistication to the most modern bath.

Bathroom Styles 53

▲ Clean lines and crisp white paint get a touch of elegance from moldings, a marble-topped vanity and the homeowner's artwork.

Most high-end homes today feature sizeable baths with plenty of space for two. These baths might also include luxurious amenities like double vanities, a separate shower and oversize tub and an enclosed toilet. These larger rooms offer a great opportunity to add a touch of panache to your home. An elegant bathroom is a feast for the eyes and a joy to the soul. But a sophisticated look doesn't have to be over-the-top—understated elegance can be achieved in myriad ways.

To start, choose darker colors for the walls, then add marble surfaces and gilded fixtures. How much further you want to take your design starts from there. Simple touches like crown molding and elegant lighting can transform any bath. Ornate custom cabinetry, elaborate window treatments and luxurious wallpaper take the look a step further. Finally, luxury options like an oversize soaking tub, featuring an array of bath salts and bubbles, complete the picture.

▲ Cherry cabinetry and wood accents create a richly luxurious look for this bathroom.

▲ A marble-topped vanity is outfitted with nickel fixtures for a look that is reminiscent of an English manor house.

◀ A marble vanity counter is a luxurious—and soothing—addition to any bathroom.

▲ A fringed valance softens the look of the tiles and marble used throughout this bath.

◀ Every touch in this bathroom—from matching picture and mirror frames to an antique cosmetics tray—lends a feeling of elegance.

Recipe for Elegance

Use these simple tips to put together a timeless scene:

• Furnish your room with handsome pieces. Transform a gracious piece of furniture into a vanity by hollowing out a spot for the sink and proper plumbing. Or if you need more counterspace, look for a vanity with room for two that has distinctive furniture-like details. Finish off the look with attractive hardware.

• Be decadent. Install two medicine cabinets, one situated above each sink. Add plenty of mirrors, perhaps ones with ornate gold frames.

• Achieve a time-honored ambiance with luxurious materials, fabrics and wallpaper. Woods like cherry and mahogany interject warmth, while marble or limestone afford texture.

• Set the mood. Interject romance with an antique or reproduction chandelier. Wall sconces with glass or cloth shades are also appropriate. For greater harmony, coordinate the finish of the sconces with the faucets and the towel bars. The finishing touch? Install dimmers so you can lessen the room's brightness when you're in the mood for a leisurely, nighttime bubble bath.

▲ Framed artwork, soft light from a table lamp and draperies over the tub are all unexpected touches of elegance in the bath.

▲ A large vanity area, inviting window seat, luxurious soaking tub and rich hickory floor all add up to an elegant bathroom sanctuary.

▲ Antique nickel faucets, fixtures and accessories are just the right complement for dark bathroom furniture, wainscotted walls and a rich wood floor.

▶ Plenty of windows give this master suite its sun-drenched look. Slatted blinds provide privacy for bathers.

▲ Black granite countertops lend restrained luxury to this elegant bath.

▲ This toilet and sink adopt the curves and lines of typical Old World architecture.

Mad for Molding

Every decorator knows that adding decorative molding and trim gives a room a finished and polished look. However, placing beautiful wood moldings in high humidity spots like bathrooms is often avoided because heat and water can cause wood to decay. Now there is a solution: Urethane millwork moldings are resistant to wood's common problems, such as decay, termites and sun damage. Choose from more than 300 molding designs, including Neoclassical and a Victorian-inspired version. Moldings can be used to great effect in the bathroom around windows, shower stalls and baths or as center rails to break up walls.

rustic

▲ Lots of natural wood and moss-colored walls give this bath a rustic feel.

If the idea of a rustic bathroom conjures up images of a quick trip outside to a chilly wooden bench—or a tiny shower stall lined with cracked linoleum—think again. Rustic does not have to mean roughing it! Bathrooms created with a rustic sensibility are all about bringing the look and feel of the great outdoors inside—without sacrificing the tiniest bit of comfort or style.

By placing an emphasis on warm, earthy colors and natural materials, such as tumbled marble, local stone and wood, rustic bathrooms bring the best of the outside world right into your own home. Rich colors and fixtures that look like they were handcrafted make the room seem like a cozy cocoon. Finishing touches such as earthen pots, lots of greenery and a carpet thrown over a tumbled marble floor can reinforce the coziness. If you're lucky enough to be secluded from your neighbors, large windows that offer views of sky, trees and wildlife are the icing on the cake.

▲ Surrounding the tub with a wide rim gives you a spot to display plants and collectibles.

▲ For a rustic feel in your bath, opt for a richly grained wood species like hickory, as in the cabinetry shown here.

Storage Solutions

Think outside the box when it comes to what you're using for storage containers. Planning decorating details right down to the smallest touches will lend a rustic flavor to your bath. Use vintage wooden trays for accessories and makeup, wicker baskets for toilet paper and towels, or even weathered flowerpots for housing bath and grooming supplies.

◀ Gleaming chrome faucets and a stainless-steel vanity bowl play against the rich matte texture of soapstone countertops.

▲ This spacious bathroom features an extensive storage system that makes efficient use of every inch of space, including cubbies for towels or makeup.

◄ This bathroom gets a touch of color from the terra-cotta tiles on the floor.

STYLE NOTES

Caddy Corner

An across-the-tub caddy, which can extend to fit the width you need, conveniently holds soap, washcloths and more—and it's a great item to have around if you're a fan of long baths. Use it to hold your favorite book while you soak.

Far from boring or run-of-the-mill, a simple, scaled-down look can be truly beautiful, conveying a sense of lightness, cleanliness and serenity. A pared-down room naturally promotes relaxation—which makes it the perfect design style for the bath.

Fixtures and surfaces in the simple bathroom are humble and unadorned. For instance, instead of including a separate tub and shower, you might opt for an all-in-one unit lined with white, square ceramic tiles. A frameless glass shower door also conjures openness, which is ideal for a smaller room.

To further enhance tranquility and a sense of harmony, enlist a monochromatic scheme, from tiles to fixtures to accessories like towels and window treatments. A simple design also relies heavily on order, so you'll want to keep clutter at bay—and out of sight. Some good storage ideas for a simple bathroom include stashing supplies in an unobtrusive vanity or a sleek medicine cabinet that is built flush to the wall.

▶ A frameless tempered-glass shower enclosure minimizes bulk, opens the look of the room and lets in light from the shower window. A simply crafted door handle complements the restrained style.

▲ Clean lines and a simple design gives this bathroom uncomplicated appeal.

▲ Basic pedestal sinks and straightforward designs—like the simply framed mirrors—lend this bathroom an understated appeal.

◀ The clean lines of this pedestal sink are echoed in the mirror and glass shelf above.

▲ With its crisp, clean styling, this mostly white bathroom is simple without being stark.

▲ This luxurious concrete soaking tub is 30 inches deep—about twice as deep as a standard tub. Large pocket windows help blur the line between outside and inside.

If you are looking for a luxurious little getaway to recharge and renew body, soul and sanity after a nonstop day, the answer might be closer than you think. Carefully planned, well-appointed "at-home spas" are the latest trend in bath design, offering you a serene and tranquil space for pampering in the comfort and privacy of your own home.

Topping the list of the most sought-after home-spa features are steam showers, exercise areas, fireplaces, soaking tubs, heated floors and luxurious "hydro-walls," where at the touch of a button, sheets of water softly cascade over opaque glass to create privacy.

Planning It Out

Of course, this kind of peaceful retreat takes a little more planning than the average bathroom redesign. To start planning your retreat, consider the space you have, as well as the amenities you want to include. Generally, a home spa offers a space for grooming and hygiene, along with areas devoted to relaxation or exercise, depending upon your individual preferences. Consider the number of people who might be using the space at any given time. For example, perhaps you enjoy yoga and meditating first thing in the morning, while your partner likes waking up with a brisk run on the treadmill. In that case, you might consider separating areas and functions of your retreat with glass walls, half-walls or screens to preserve privacy and tranquility.

▲ Treat yourself to a spa treatment in your own home with a whirlpool tub.

Glass Act

Wise homeowners take note: Glass block is back, and it has a brand-new attitude. Do you have a layout problem like windows that are too close to a neighbor? Need your shower to jut into the room—without seeming like it was just plopped there? Need privacy in a bath shared with a spouse? In each case, glass block is the solution. Its contemporary good looks are ideal for providing privacy from passersby outside while still admitting plenty of sunlight. And there's nothing better for creating a stunning shower that's translucent yet not transparent. Finally, in a small bath, consider using glass block to create a compartment for the toilet that won't make you feel like you're locked in a closet.

▲ A luxurious, oversize tub or whirlpool deserves a luxurious, oversize tub filler. The graceful arc of the one shown here repeats the arch of the opening of the bathing nook.

For most, the simplicity, balance and constant regeneration found in nature offer an inspired source of renewal. Bringing the outside in or opening up your retreat to the outdoors reinforces your relationship with the natural world and captures the essence of the spa experience. If you are able to incorporate this element, you can do so by using doors or sliding window walls that open onto a private garden.

Even if you can't go that far, whenever possible, take advantage of surrounding gardens, landscapes or panoramic vistas to set the natural tone of your spa. If you are limited by space, budget and access to the outdoors, consider adding a small fountain, plants or a garden statue to replicate the look and feel of the outdoors.

Picking Palette & Materials

Organic, earthy materials and soft watery colors establish a soothing palette. Honed sandstone, travertine, limestone and translucent marbles provide texture and depth in neutral tones for floors and countertops. Wood cabinetry and trim, in complementary hues, build upon the natural theme.

▶ An oversize shower lined with soothing beige tiles provides a luxurious escape from the everyday.

▲ In this bath, naturally textured elements, like the slate floor and mosaic tiles, provide a welcome contrast to the smooth wall tiles.

◀ Surrounding this soaking tub with wood introduces a look that's a cross between an Asian tea room and a Scandinavian sauna.

Complete Your Retreat

Once your meticulous planning and hard work have transformed your dream bath into a beautiful reality, it's time to enjoy your special sanctuary. However, before you dip your toes into your long-awaited lavender-scented bath, why not grace your space with a few of the finishing touches that professional spas use to pamper their patrons?

• Keep a generous supply of plush, oversize bath towels in wicker baskets next to the tub, shower or exercise area.

• Use plenty of ornamental hooks throughout your master bath to keep fluffy terry cloth robes conveniently within arm's reach.

• Install a music system to fill your retreat with soft music or the gentle sounds of nature.

• Splurge on an original painting or sculpture by your favorite artist to gaze upon while you soak. Just make sure the piece is protected from moisture damage.

• Consider adding a small refrigerator stocked with mineral water or iced herb tea for sipping while relaxing.

• To soften skin and soothe weary muscles, treat yourself to a fragrant selection of French-milled soaps and aromatherapy lotions and bath oils.

◀ A large mirror enhances the sense of space and doubles the vistas in this bathroom. A limestone countertop lends cohesiveness and also serves as an eye-catching contrast to the shiny steel sink.

▲ To achieve a truly deep soak, you'll need a tub that fills all the way to the brim. Lots of windows showcasing a glorious landscape complete the feeling of escape in this bath.

▲ A wall of mirrors above the vanity reflects the natural light that's abundant in this room. Pale tile, cabinets and surfacing reinforce the airy effect.

▲ By angling the tub and separating the his-and-her vanities, the architect who designed this bathroom cleverly made way for all the amenities in the 250-square-foot room.

▲ Five body shower jets and a showerhead that adjusts from an invigorating spray to a drenching flow helps transform an ordinary bathroom into a relaxing retreat.

▶ Multiple body jets in the shower and a heated towel rack add to a spalike experience.

STYLE NOTES

Mix It Up

Mixing materials is one of the strongest trends when it comes to bathroom design. Below, we offer a few tips from the pros:

• Texture, which is perhaps the most overlooked element in interior design, lends a space as much visual interest as color and pattern do—but in a subtle, understated manner. Try mixing tactile surfaces—like slightly rough slate tiles on the floor and a tub surround with smooth, glass-block shower walls—with a large expanse of mirror. A space covered in shiny ceramic tiles might call for a matte-finished sink or textured wallcoverings, for example, to provide contrast.

• Monochromatic spaces tend to produce a more relaxing look, but that doesn't mean you can't use color for dramatic impact. To achieve depth, choose tiles with a natural range of coloration.

• When adding patterns to your design scheme, it's usually best to avoid busy ones or even something as tailored as a bold stripe. Instead, use architectural patterns like a grid of a glass-block wall or a tile backsplash to create the dynamic style your space requires.

vintage

▲ Each decorating detail—from the claw-foot tub to the casement windows to the toiletries on the wicker stand—lends this bathroom a timeless appeal.

An older house is a treasure to be protected and very often features design elements that you will want to preserve. A vintage bath, for example, features classic elements that hearken back to a simpler time, such as pedestal sinks, graceful chrome fittings and substantial moldings and millwork. But although you might want to preserve the vintage look of your bathroom, you'll certainly want to update all the fixtures and amenities. Luckily, you can have the best of both worlds.

For an old-fashioned look in a new space, it's important to focus on the details. It's easy enough to add baseboard and crown moldings or even beadboard paneling that stretches to chair-rail height. Small touches, like unlacquered brass fittings that will mellow into a soft patina over time, can give a newly remodeled bath antique appeal. Finally, painted wood cabinets topped with marble and reproduction light fixtures add graceful finishing touches.

▲ Every detail is right in this vintage reproduction—from the light fixtures to the elegant shaving utensils and crystal-cut perfume bottles on the his-and-her vanities.

▲ The graceful etching that frames this mirror is a subtle detail that exemplifies the fine craftsmanship that was typical of homes built early in the twentieth century.

◀ Over time, the finish on this tub filler will mellow into an antiqued look.

▲ White fixtures, tile and wainscoting have a timeless appeal. Small gestures like the shower seat render the room more functional without marring its tenor.

◀ Instead of flowing from a faucet, water in this sink comes out through a lip at the rear of the basin. The faucet and valves mounted on the wall above are solely decorative.

▲ This vintage-looking shower control is outside the stall, so you won't risk getting scalded while adjusting the temperature.

▲ Glass mosaic tiles in soft greens and deep browns are paired with a carved stone border for a rich, inviting look that's a perfect complement to the marble vanity countertop.

Taking a Stand

Although built-in cabinets are still prevalent in many baths, there's a strong trend toward the "unfitted" look you can achieve by using freestanding cabinets and cupboards. Interiors furnished with these items have a very vintage look that recalls the Hoosier cabinets beloved by our grandmothers and favored by antique collectors for their practicality. Many custom and semicustom cabinetry collections include unfitted pieces, so shop around.

▲ Painted wood cabinets are topped with marble to mimic the charm of an old-fashioned bath.

DETAILS, DETAILS, DETAILS

◀ A simply styled vanity topped with polished green slate offers a clean, crisp look in this mostly white bath.

bathroom
cabinets

▲ This cabinet with rope molding, shown in cherry with a vanilla glaze, is also available in a variety of finishes for oak, maple and hickory hardwoods and several softwoods.

In most cases, the bathroom is the smallest room in the house. Paradoxically, it generally serves as a depository for lots and lots of stuff. From makeup to shaving supplies to toothbrushes, the bathroom houses the products we buy to pamper ourselves and create a spa experience in our humble bath. So where can we store all our goodies, as well as toilet paper and cleaning supplies? A vanity may be the answer.

When you start designing your bath, you'll find that the cabinetry will become one of the most predominant elements of the space. The style, material and finish will determine the look of your room. And, in all likelihood, the cabinetry will be your biggest expense. Therefore, you'll want to know all of your options before you make any decisions. And remember: Whatever material you choose, look inside the vanity as well. Many of today's units include such features as one- and two-tier drawer organizers; pull-out towel holders; pull-out and tilt-out laundry bins; wire baskets in various sizes and depths; revolving shelves; and under-counter tip-out tray systems. To figure out what look is right for you, you'll need to focus on what you like and dislike. To do this, flip through magazines, study design books and visit bath showrooms to find your favorite style.

▲ Brighten up your bath—and your day—by taking advantage of the rainbow of colored cabinet finishes available today.

Spotting the Trends

Over the last few years, three strong trends have emerged in bath and, accordingly, cabinet design.

The spa bath. With our desire to take a break from the fast pace of our daily lives, a spalike bath offers a calming refuge. Pale colors, natural materials and lots of white all contribute to this cool, comforting atmosphere. Try, for example, a light maple vanity topped with a glass counter surrounded by white walls. These elements may be just what you need to transform your bath into a sybaritic retreat.

The furniture look. Recently there has been a return to the historic styles of baths equipped with furniture rather than built-in cabinets. You can achieve this look in a vanity cabinet by adding furniture legs or bun feet, relief carvings on door panels and natural stone or wood countertops. You may find a Victorian- or mission-style cabinet to match the architectural style of your house and transform it into a vanity.

But if you choose this route, you should be sure the cabinet has proper cutouts to accommodate plumbing and fittings. You'll also want to measure carefully to make sure the piece will fit through your doors.

The hip hotel. Why not have a bath that will make you feel like you are staying in a trendy boutique hotel? To outfit your chic bath, select a metal vanity with, say, a curved front cabinet and an above-counter sink set on a glass or stone countertop.

▲ A look that has been gaining popularity of late pairs an above-counter sink with a stone or other natural material countertop. This particular style and size vanity offers plenty of counterspace for everyday grooming essentials.

▲ This vanity, with its classic lines, clean silhouettes and fresh white finish, adds an updated simplicity to a chic bathroom suite.

▲ This line of cabinetry includes vanities that are 35 inches tall—that's five inches taller than standard height—for added comfort and increased storage.

Getting Down to It

The materials you choose for your vanity will affect not only its appearance but also its durability and price—it makes sense to stick to the basics. You can quickly and easily change the look of your bathroom with different towels, wall color and hardware, but you may eventually tire of a purple countertop. What looks avant-garde and hip today may look absurd tomorrow.

In terms of cabinets, there are many good options. If you want durability, wood cabinets may be the answer. These can be painted if they are prop-erly primed and finished with a good sealer to protect against humidity. Plastic laminates, which are less costly than woods, probably won't last as long as wood but may still outlive you. For an industrial look, consider metal. It provides a sleek look but will require specialized cleaning care.

Materials and Finishes

Surprisingly, few cabinets today are made of solid wood. Top-of-the-line cabinets often have solid wood doors (though veneers or high-pressure lami-nates also can be superior quality), but not solid wood cabinet boxes, which have a tendency to warp and twist. Painted cabinetry is often constructed of a close-grained wood such as maple or poplar and is often treated with a chip-resistant thermofoil process. The majority of cabinets are constructed of plywood or composite-board boxes covered with wood veneers. Some manufacturers also offer metal cabi-nets, usually formulated with steel doors and composite-board boxes. Finishes to consider include the popu-lar new glazes, anything distressed and soft color washes for a farmhouse look.

▼ Classic off-white, raised-panel cabinets bridge the gap between up-to-the-minute bathroom amenities and a look of old-fashioned luxury.

Small Spaces

Bathrooms may have gotten bigger in the last decade, but many are still the standard 6 feet by 9 feet. To make the most of limited space, install floor-to-ceiling cabinetry. This uses the full height of the room to its best advantage. Also, adding a shelf about a foot below the ceiling around the perimeter of the room is a great way to get items off the vanity top.

▲ Built-in cabinetry includes drawers and cupboard space to keep things organized.

▲ Constructed of furniture-quality dark solid oak, this vanity features a unique door design that would work beautifully in an Arts and Crafts-style home or one that has an Old World style.

▲ Oak-beaded, raised-panel cabinetry offers true elegance with its decoratively carved scrolled corbel. It's shown here in solid wood for the dressing table.

Selecting Style & Substance

If you want a sleek look, you'll probably be drawn to frameless, or Eurostyle, cabinets. The doors on frameless units are flush with the outer edge of the cabinet boxes, creating a smooth, contemporary appearance. This construction is ideal for laminates and veneers. To warm up a contemporary bath, consider a wood veneer like maple. If you want to really dazzle your friends, pick a brightly hued laminate. Since the design and color of laminates come from a photographic image that is then bonded to other layers, the choices are quite diverse.

No matter what type of cabinetry you ultimately select, make sure you examine each of the units for signs of quality craftsmanship. For superior durability, interconnected joints, such as dovetails, hold together without nails. The next best options are connections that have a structural bridge: doweled or biscuit joints, for example. Simple butt or lap joints may work themselves loose over time, especially if they're stapled. Examine the drawers, looking for glides that open all the way quietly and smoothly while keeping the drawer horizontal even when fully extended.

Comparing Prices

There are three different "levels" of bathroom cabinet. As with anything else, the more control you want over the look of your cabinetry, the more it's going to cost!

Stock units are the most reasonably priced cabinetry, but they are less adaptable than custom or semicustom units. You'll have to combine stock parts of a modular system to fit your space, so some units might not fit—you could end up with a few extra inches that will need to be bridged with fillers. Luckily any designer or architect assisting you with your project will have no

▼ The right vanity can bring the entire bath to life. This understated vanity, with its refreshingly simple lines, keeps the look of your bathroom light.

▲ Frameless cabinetry has a seamless look and distinctive modern lines.

problem overcoming this obstacle. And unlike custom or semicustom cabinets, stock units arrive quickly.

The next level of cost is semicustom cabinets. These are almost as flexible as custom cabinets but are available at a midrange price point. Made mainly of stock components, these units also have added custom features—the cabinet dealer can assemble the pieces for a truly custom look.

The most expensive option is cabinetry that is custom designed and built to fit your room. Though most commonly used in kitchens, custom cabinets can add extra elegance to the bath.

▲ Architectural moldings with dentil accents add interest to this custom bathroom cabinetry, which includes a vanity and plenty of extra storage.

▲ Traditional elegance is reflected in this vanity with raised-panel doors. The look is completed by flanking cabinets featuring glass-front doors and recessed lighting.

▲ This vanity offers plenty of functional storage. It includes a pull-out tray, built-in grooming rack and other features that help keep clutter off the countertop.

▲ There's nothing like custom cabinetry for getting exactly the look you want for your room. This suite, which evokes the Orient, is crafted in oak with ebony accents.

▲ Though this cabinetry looks like it was custom built for the room, it's really semicustom. With so many options available, you won't need to spend a fortune to get the look you want.

One of the easiest and least expensive ways to "dress up" your new bathroom vanity is by adding decorative door and drawer pulls and knobs. In fact, even if you've chosen to keep your old vanity, simply updating the hardware can have the entire unit looking good as new. Many cabinetry manufacturers offer a variety of hardware choices with each vanity they produce. There is also a wide array of knobs and pulls that you can buy independently of your bathroom furniture.

Feeling whimsical? Try ceramic knobs painted with flowers. Want to get back to nature? Go with wood or metal pulls. No matter what your mood, there's something to fit your personality to a tee. When making your selection, though, keep a few practical considerations in mind. Cabinet handles and drawer pulls should be easy to use and easy to clean. Smooth, round designs are safer than angular or sharp pieces, especially if there are children in the house.

▲ This vanity—inspired by furniture designs from a more romantic time—brings antique elegance to your bath.

▲ New door and drawer pulls are a simple way to refresh your bath without spending a fortune. With hundreds of style options—from handmade knobs with a textural, rustic look to glass knobs reminiscent of cabinet hardware from the 1920s and '30s—you're sure to find something that suits your taste.

◀ Simple, luxurious stone surfacing is one of the easiest ways to give your bath an air of timeless elegance.

stunning
surfaces

▲ Long a designer favorite, concrete is coming into its own in high-style baths. The silky-smooth surface belies the material's industrial-quality strength and durability. And when it comes to form, color and texture, the possibilities are unlimited.

nspired by nature and improved by technology, today's surfacing options add all-around style to the bath. What you select for your walls, floors and counters will certainly set the mood of your room.

Whether you are preparing to meet the world or are trying to escape from it, you deserve a space that soothes and rejuvenates your soul. In this day and age of career and family obligations, when you are left with little time for solitude, the bath may be the only place where you can relax. When shopping for the surfacing elements for your new retreat, insist on top-of-the-line materials, reliable performance and excellent value.

Today, the hottest looks for bathroom surfaces represent a mixture of yin and yang. Combining smooth and rough textures, shiny and dull finishes and colorful and clear materials makes a style statement that will set your bath apart. Surfaces tend to be lighter overall in the bath, as this room is meant to be a relaxing oasis—a place for quiet escape and reflection. Of course, that doesn't mean you can't incorporate a rich blend of materials and textures here. With a working palette that runs from natural stone, metallic laminates and translucent mosaic glass for countertops to wallpaper, textured paints and ceramic tiles for the walls, it's easy to mix and match.

▲ When it comes to selecting a color for your bathroom counters, black might not be the first one that springs to mind. But dark counters, like this quartz surfacing, can make a bold statement.

More so than any other room in the house, the bathroom is designed to work hard. Though every fixture in this room will see repeated use every day, no other element will take the beating your countertops will. The sink or vanity top sees a little bit of everything—from soap scum and grime to hairspray and makeup—so you'll want to choose your materials with care. Luckily, the products available today are not only constructed of top-quality, long-lasting materials, they're

also stunning design elements in their own right. Following is a quick primer of what's out there.

Solid Surfacing

Solid surfacing has become a mainstay in both the kitchen and bath. Earning its name from the fact that the grain goes all the way through, solid surfacing can be cut, drilled and routed like wood. The resulting design flexibility, along with the material's durability and low-maintenance requirements, makes

it a popular choice for bathroom counters. Solid surfacing is generally crafted of plastic resins that are bound by adhesives and mineral fillers that give the product its color and flame resistance. The result is a "solid" block of material that is both durable and nonporous. Solid-surfacing applications are also manufactured to the exact specifications of each job, so they are completely seamless. The nonporous nature of the surface, combined with this seamless application, makes it very hygienic—bacteria and mold have nowhere here to collect and grow. Finally, because the color is consistent all the way through, any imperfections that arise from daily use of the countertop can be sanded out.

Solid surfacing is a very popular choice in new homes and remodeled spaces because it is extremely versatile and offers seemingly unlimited potential for applications. Integrated and drop-in sinks, which are seamlessly bound to the adjacent countertop, are also fairly typical in today's remodeled rooms. However, the possibilities for incorporating solid surfacing into your rooms can extend far beyond these standard applications. And because every job is made to the specifications of a unique countertop design, they are all essentially custom creations.

The choices of color in solid surfacing are as endless as those for applications. Shades of white are still the most popular choice, but manufacturers also offer patterns that mimic natural materials like concrete, granite and terrazzo. Bold interpretations that take advantage of the unlimited potential of this synthetic material include bright colors and those that are almost translucent. Some of the most popular new trends are in the so-called "large particulate" patterns, which feature chunky tone-on-tone flecks.

To complete the picture, solid surfacing is available in a variety of finishes. While a glossy surface is the most common, a honed, or matte, finish is also available—as is semigloss.

▲ This solid-surfacing vanity and countertop blend perfectly with the overall traditional styling of this bathroom.

▲ To give your solid-surfacing counters a little extra personality, consider adding a detailed edge treatment like the two-tone look shown here.

▲ This line of solid surfacing comes in a choice of 23 colors. The dark countertop used on this vanity adds a richness to the wood cabinet below.

Stone

Which countertop material offers timeless beauty and appeal, is easy on the environment, requires relatively little maintenance, works hard and will last a lifetime? The answer is easy—and gorgeous: stone. If you're not sure which type of stone will best suit your needs, practically and stylistically, you can learn about each of the most common choices here.

Granite is available in an array of colors, including blacks, golds, blues, greens and grays. Extremely hard and heat- and stain-resistant, granite can be finished with either a polished or a matte surface.

Marble is softer than granite in both density and appearance, and, therefore, is particularly susceptible to scratching. As such, it is usually reserved for use in the bath. Like granite, marble comes in a range of colors—whites, yellows, creams and browns—and patterns. Typically, marble varieties with less veining and a more uniform appearance will cost a bit more.

Though it is soft, soapstone is more resistant to staining than most other stone materials. Composed primarily of talc, soapstone has a particularly smooth surface and colors, ranging from blue to gray, that will darken over time. There is one special consideration for using soapstone: It must be sealed periodically with mineral oil, not a commercial sealant.

Limestone, available in whites, yellows, browns, grays and blacks, features a soft, mellow appearance. Rather porous, it needs regular sealing to prevent staining. Because the density of limestone depends on the variety, some scratch more easily than others.

Slate appeals to homeowners with rustic tastes because of its matte surface and irregular split face. Available in a range of colors, including purples, reds, greens and grays, a slate countertop can be sanded with steel wool to remove scratches.

▼ This vanity top and sink, both of which are crafted from marble, form one continuous piece.

Crystal Clear Choice

Quartz composite countertops are similar in composition to solid surfacing, but actually include real quartz crystals that are bound together with an adhesive. The surface resists scratches, burns and stains and, like solid surfacing, requires no sealing. The quartz crystals that compose the material, however, give it a depth and clarity not seen in other materials, particularly synthetic ones. Color choices include whites, reds, blues, blacks and more. Many edge treatments are available, and the counters come in ¾-inch and 1⅛-inch thicknesses. Manufacturers typically offer a 10-year warranty.

▲ Cutting corners takes on new meaning with countertop materials like marble. Today you can forgo the traditional rectangle and really customize the look of your bath.

▲ Granite, which can be used everywhere from floors to countertops to walls, lends a sophisticated air to the bath.

Concrete

For a stone alternative that isn't really stone think concrete. Concrete countertops (and floors) are hand troweled in molds, cast and diamond polished for a finish similar to honed granite. If you're looking for a material that's truly eco-friendly, the ultimate "green" countertop is Syndecrete, a mixture of fly-ash concrete and recycled bits of glass, plastic and metal.

Laminate

Affordable and attractive, plastic laminate is the most popular option for the bath. It is made by fusing decorative paper to layers of resin-saturated Kraft paper under high heat and pressure and then bonding the surface to particleboard or plywood. You'll find just about every color, pattern and texture you can imagine in this material. The most popular patterns are neutrals that mimic natural materials like stone, though bright colors and other options are also available. You can also give laminate an upgraded look with special edge treatments, including aluminum.

Laminate is waterproof and easy to clean. But since the color does not go all the way through the material, cuts and nicks will show over time. Unfortunately, laminate cannot be repaired, it can only be replaced.

▲ This integrated sink and countertop help make cleanup a snap.

▼ This quartz surfacing incorporates semiprecious stones into the surface for a unique look.

Keeping Your New Countertops Clean

Nothing makes a bathroom look better than shining surfaces. Here are the best ways to keep a variety of countertops clean:

• Solid surfacing. Clean with soapy water. Gentle sanding with a mild abrasive pad or cleanser will remove stains or scratches. Some spray cleaners may discolor the surface, so check with the manufacturer for recommended products.

• Granite. Wipe with a mild dish detergent or sanitize with a solution of diluted bleach as needed. Abrasive cleansers can damage or stain the surface. Reseal every two years.

• Marble, limestone, soapstone and concrete. Make sure your installer applies a food-safe, penetrating sealer. To clean, wipe down with hot, soapy water.

• Laminate. Wipe surface as needed with a damp cloth and a mild liquid detergent. Do not use abrasive cleaners, which can scratch the surface. Use a nylon-bristled brush and mild cleanser to remove stubborn stains.

▲ Sleek and sophisticated, this integrated sink—counter and bowl—is available in more than 20 shades of lacquered glass.

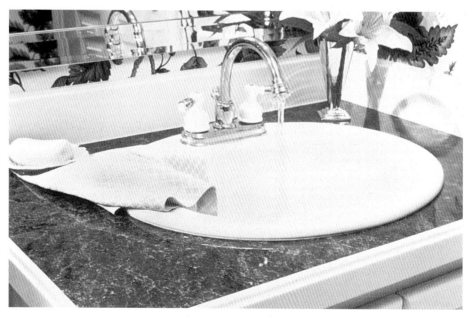

▲ A bordered counter gives a polished look to this bath, while the laminate surface provides a dash of color and works well with the brass faucet.

walls

▲ Wallpaper is ideal for playing up architectural features like interesting moldings. Here, a pattern of delicate starfish dancing across a neutral background keeps the atmosphere light.

As you get ready to cover your walls, you need to consider a few things, including your personality. If you're someone who likes to change the look of your bath frequently, consider wallpaper or paint rather than tile. If you definitely want tile, pick a neutral color—this way you can easily change the look of your interior just by switching the accessories, like window treatments, towels and the shower curtain. No matter what look you're going for, you'll need to do some research

before you make any decisions. For starters, you'll want to select low-maintenance materials. Tile, stone, paint and wallpaper are all excellent choices for bathroom walls. Keep in mind that larger tiles require less grout than small ones (like mosaics), making it easier to keep walls clean. If you select paint or wallpaper for your bathroom walls, make sure your choice is mildew resistant and designed for use in high-moisture areas. Whether you go for tile, wallpaper or a fresh coat of

paint, the most important thing to remember when covering your walls is that today's look is all about creating a space that is uniquely yours.

Wallpaper

No design element sets a tone or personalizes a room like wallpaper can. Today's wallcoverings, available in an abundant assortment of designs, colors, tones and textures, are a wonderful way to breathe new life into your bath in as little as an afternoon. If it's

▲ The soft-hued flowers gracing the walls give this bath the air of a country cottage.

▲ Today's elegant master suites call for equally elegant wallcoverings. A rich pattern like this one will help you create a truly eye-catching retreat.

been a while since you peeked inside a wallpaper sample book, you're in for a pleasant surprise. You'll find marvelous new looks, fresh colors and interesting textures that were unheard of just a few years ago. Today's look features realistic, nature-inspired textured papers that add beauty and depth to a room by simulating bamboo, granite and wood grains in subtle earth tones. Remember grass cloth? It's back, but this time in metallic copper and gold. Also gaining popularity are hand-screened papers and those that replicate faux finishes. Artistically inspired murals and trompe l'oeil wallcoverings, too, are an easy and fun way to create visual interest.

In terms of color, once again, earth tones and deep neutrals like mocha and taupe set the mood in many of today's popular papers. You'll also see plenty of warm reds and rich terra-cottas, plus an assortment of cool tones, such as light blue, aqua and lavender.

Choosing the Right Paper

Selecting paper for the bath requires a little more thought than other rooms. You'll need to use a vinyl paper that's sturdy enough to withstand the humidity, heat and temperature changes common to the area. Since most papers found on the market today fall into this category, you'll have an enormous range from which to choose. Then consider your family's lifestyle in selecting a paper with attributes that fit your needs. An excellent choice for baths are scrubbable papers that are designed to withstand mildly abrasive brushes and detergents. Washable papers are those that may be sponged clean to remove fingerprints and grime. Colorfast wallcoverings resist fading when exposed to sunlight, and strippable wallpaper is easily peeled from the wall, leaving behind minimal paste and residue. Prepasted means that the paper has been treated with a water-activated adhesive, making it easier to hang.

Selecting a Pattern

When you are ready to start shopping for a wallpaper pattern, you should look everywhere and anywhere for inspiration—and keep these few tips in mind. Geometric patterns, including plaids and stripes, create a dramatic look that draws the eye upward, making your ceilings appear higher. Large prints make an oversize room appear smaller and more intimate, while small prints add visual interest and background color to open up cramped rooms or tiny spaces. Finally, overall color, including solids and textures, creates a cohesive background that establishes a unified setting. Of course, as with any decorating decision, the most important consideration when choosing your paper is how it will look in your home. Never purchase any wallcovering without first looking at a sample in your home, where lighting and other room elements may affect your decision.

▼ Wallpaper is a perfect way to indulge your sense of whimsy. Whether you're a gardener or a collector of porcelain, you'll find a pattern or border that reflects your personality.

Update with Paper

A versatile assortment of prepasted, ready-to-hang decorative papers, borders and trompe l'oeil panels can quickly and easily add visual interest to any room. Some ideas include creating a room with a "view" by adding a scenic "window" panel, waking up a sleepy nook with trompe l'oeil or applying a classical border 36 inches from the floor to replicate architectural molding—for a fraction of the cost. You can also apply a similar border 6 to 12 inches down from the ceiling. For overall interest, consider a textural paper like the stone-wall look shown above.

▲ Texture is the latest thing in wallpaper—here a sidewall papered with an almond and blue scroll design gives the walls rich three-dimensionality.

▲ If pale neutrals and watery hues are not for you, consider something a little more daring. This richly flowered wallcovering makes a great statement—especially when it's paired with simple white tiles and fixtures.

Painting

Picking paint can be a lengthy process. Before you begin, think about the other colors you'll be using in your bathroom—from window treatments to the vanity to the towels. Remember these elements when you go to the paint dealer to pick out new wall colors. Think about the effect you'd like to achieve—dark colors can create a dramatic effect, but they can make a room look smaller. Paler shades generally work well in bathrooms because of the greater need for light. Earthy materials and soft watery colors establish a soothing palette that's right at home in the bath. And trims and moldings can be painted in a contrasting or coordinating color.

To help judge a color on your walls, paint a small area of the wall and live with it for a while. Look at it in daylight and artificial light. See how it coordinates or contrasts with objects in the room. When choosing bold colors, pick two shades lighter than your original choice because it becomes more intense when painted on a large surface.

Paint Types

The two basic types of paint are latex and oil. Latex dries quickly and can be cleaned up easily with soap and water; however, it is less durable than oil-based paints. Oil-based paints require more time to dry, let off more fumes and need to be cleaned up with turpentine or paint thinner.

Finishes include flat, eggshell, semigloss and high gloss. These finishes are listed in order of their sheen, with a flat paint giving the most matte finish. When deciding between finishes, keep in mind that the higher the sheen, the easier the wall will be to clean. High gloss and semigloss are best for high-traffic areas, so you'll want to use semigloss everywhere in the bathroom, including on doorframes and trims. This will make it easier to clean up after fingerprints and mildew.

▼ The wall color used in this bath makes the room feel like a tranquil oasis of calm.

Getting Ready to Paint

Before you paint, you'll need to clean the walls thoroughly. Old wallpaper needs to be removed, holes should be patched and rough spots should be sanded. To remove dust or dirt from the wall surface, wash it down before painting. For this, use TSP (trisodium phosphate) and wash from the bottom up to avoid streaking. Wear gloves to protect your hands. Rinse with clear water and a sponge. To wash off mildew, use a mixture of 1 to 2 cups of bleach per gallon of warm water. You can paint—or prime—the walls as soon as they are completely dry.

▲ The bathroom is one of the best places to try your hand at creating a faux finish: The smaller room size means your masterpiece will come together much more quickly.

▲ Soothing colors in various shades of brown are a very popular choice for the bath.

▲ Painting the walls in a soft, rosy color added a touch of warmth to this bathroom.

Tile

Practical and beautiful. Contemporary and traditional. Familiar and sometimes surprising. Those paradoxical words describe tile, the functional and decorative material that's been a part of houses both grand and modest for literally thousands of years. With properties that explain its long popularity—strength, durability, ease of care and terrific looks—there's no doubt tile will be going strong for millennia to come.

If tile already gleams on your bathroom floor and walls, you probably don't really need new coverings—with minimal upkeep, tile is likely to last at least a lifetime or two. But if you're building or renovating, or simply want a change from another material, you're in luck: Tile options have never been more abundant or exciting. Colors range from subtle natural tones to brilliant hues—in both solids and patterns. Surfaces are smooth as glass (in fact, some are glass) or textured in various ways—from overall geometric designs to incised motifs, such as leaves, flowers, fruits and vegetables, shells and sea creatures. Some are designed to mimic other materials, such as stone and slate. More than ever before, there's something to suit every house style and every homeowner's desires. And you can tailor the amount of surface you

▲ Surround yourself in leather with tiles that are sealed to resist water. They're perfect for bathroom walls, but shouldn't be used in areas with standing water.

◀ The dramatic effect in this bath comes from glass mosaic tiles. These tiny tiles create a rich, textural surface. Adding a 24-karat gold leaf trim is the ultimate in luxury.

▶ The tiles used in this bathroom feature rich motifs inspired by the heritage of the historic Hamptons in New York.

dedicate to tile according to your taste. You can add tiles in border designs, as murals or even inlaid randomly, to add new life to your room.

Whether you're considering vast expanses of tile or a few decorative additions, you probably have a good idea of the colors and kinds of patterns you want. It's equally important to take along some knowledge of tile basics. Terms can be confusing. For instance, although the word tile generally refers to ceramic tile (a mineral composition fired at a high temperature), you'll also hear about the currently popular porcelain tile and glass tile—which are ceramics too, but

specifically named for their content. To compound any confusion, there are stone, marble and concrete tiles, so called because the materials have been cut in traditional tile shapes. As for the metallic tiles that are making a splash right now, most are ceramic tiles with a metallic finish added after firing.

Tiles come in various degrees of hardness determined by the minerals of which they're made. Those that rank above center on the industry's one-to-ten hardness scale were made to hold up to the impact of heavy foot traffic, while those lower on the scale are suitable for walls. With careful installation, floor tiles can be used successfully on

walls (or anywhere), but the reverse is generally not true. Glazed tiles are those to which color, mixed with a glassy substance, has been applied before firing. In the kiln, the glaze melts and forms a hard top coat. Depending on the composition of the glaze, the finished tile can be either shiny or matte. In unglazed tiles, the color—which may be the natural color of the mineral or one created with mixed-in pigments—is all through the tile body. Although unglazed tiles emerge from the kiln with a matte finish, they can be polished, if you prefer that look, with special equipment, in the same process that's used for polishing natural stone.

▼ Take advantage of the many decorative accessories available with most of today's ceramic tile collections for a simple look that's anything but stark and chilly.

Filling in the Spaces

Grout, also known as joint filler, is more than an aesthetic finishing touch. It's necessary to keep dirt from lodging between the installed tiles. According to the Tile Council of America, there are three kinds of grout available today:

• Cement grout (sometimes with color added). This is the least expensive grout. Unsealed, it discolors easily and, because it is porous, it absorbs water and stains from spills. To avoid these problems, it's important to use a sealer, which is available from tile distributors, after the cement has cured.

• Latex-added cement grout. The latex ingredient gives the grout some flexibility to expand and contract, as well as some stain resistance.

• Epoxy grout. The hardness and strength of this product assure superior resistance to stains and cracking. It costs more than the others, and because application is a two-part process, installation also costs more.

▲ Subway tile is popular in bathrooms and includes a variety of wall tiles and moldings. The different patterns used in this bathroom combine beautifully with each other and the counter.

▲ The owner of this bathroom brought an underwater effect to the room by choosing small tiles in a variety of blue and green hues.

▲ Bring the beautiful, rich look of wood into the bath. Thanks to advanced sealing systems, many laminate floors are now safe for use in higher moisture areas.

There's no getting around it: The bathroom floor is one of the most utilitarian items in the house. But that doesn't mean it can't look great while it works! From vinyl to stone to laminate, there's a floor style for every taste—and budget. When you're shopping for a floor, give your creativity free reign. More and more, manufacturers and homeowners are experimenting with patterns, borders and insets. With vinyl tile floors, for example, you can easily create a look that's unique to your home by the way in which you place and combine the tiles. You can also consider mixing materials, such as wood and stone. Not sure where to start? Read on.

Vinyl

If you are searching for a flooring product that is low maintenance and won't break the bank, you should definitely consider vinyl. The resilient surface of vinyl flooring makes it easy on the feet and back. Even better, a dropped glass or makeup compact is much less likely to shatter when it hits a vinyl floor as opposed to harder flooring materials like tile or stone.

Today's options are affordable and better than ever. Gone are the ho-hum patterns you may remember from your grandmother's bathroom. Vinyl flooring manufacturers now offer high-style choices—from designs that imitate the look and feel of ceramic tile, wood and stone to floors that feature a metallic effect.

▲ This vinyl no-wax tile has a subtle geometric pattern that features the shape of a diamond with a scrolled border within the square tile. The tile also has a stonelike texture.

▲ Today's vinyl flooring has a lot to offer— it's springy underfoot, water-resistant, easy to clean and affordable.

▲ These tiles offer rustic appeal and feature a no-wax surface that's simple to clean.

There are two basic methods of applying pattern and texture to vinyl flooring: rotogravure, in which the pattern is printed on the surface, and inlay, in which the pattern goes all the way through the material. Inlaid vinyl is generally more expensive. Both types must be installed over a smooth, hard, dry, level surface.

In addition to a choice of color, texture and pattern, you have the choice of using sheet vinyl or vinyl tiles. Sheet vinyl is more popular for larger spaces because it offers a seamless look, which makes it simple to keep clean. But if you decide to replace the floor later, sheet vinyl cannot be removed as easily as other floorings. See if your pattern is available in a perimeter bond application before you opt for the full spread. Perimeter bond is only glued at walls and seams. After installation the flooring shrinks to tighten over the floor.

Linoleum, which is made from a mixture of linseed oil, ground cork, wood flour, rosin and color pigments applied to a jute backing, is a natural alternative to vinyl flooring. Stain-resistant linoleum should last 15 years or more. If you plan to use linoleum in a bathroom, however, keep in mind that the seams must be heat welded, as exposure to excessive water can cause bubbling and expansion.

Laminate

Manufacturers of laminate flooring will tell you that their product is stain resistant, impact resistant, easy to clean and relatively inexpensive. It's a durable flooring choice for households with active lifestyles, particularly when used in kitchens, hallways and family rooms. But only recently have some manufacturers given their products the green light for use in bathrooms.

A low-maintenance material that provides the look of wood or tile, plastic laminate flooring is made of resin-impregnated paper bonded to high-density fiberboard and protected by a clear wearlayer. Sold in planks, squares

▼ Tile is beautiful, but if you have a lot of floor space, you may come to dread maintaining all that grout. Instead, try faux tile laminate floors. The look is ceramic, but the upkeep is easy.

▲ There are few more elegant flooring looks than that of timeworn stone. You can get the same effect with laminates like this one.

◀ Gleaming black flooring complements the black counter and cherry vanity in this bath.

and blocks, it effectively gives the look of many different types of wood, stone and tile flooring. Laminate is easily installed over an existing level floor and resists most scratches and stains.

Though some companies claim their products are capable of standing up to the moist conditions of a bathroom, most laminate flooring manufacturers warn that prolonged exposure to standing water will harm the surface. Most flooring specialists agree that installing laminate floors in powder rooms and seldom-used guest baths is not a problem. But before you go with laminate for a heavy-use bathroom, make sure the manufacturer recommends it for high-moisture conditions. Laminate flooring is properly installed with water-resistant glue (instead of the white glue that is commonly used) and should come with a water-damage warranty from the manufacturer.

Tile

Tile has been around for many centuries, in a variety of applications and in all kinds of buildings, so it might seem that it's architecturally old hat—especially in the bathroom. But that is far from the truth. Designs in tile always look fresh and new, making it as exciting a choice right now as it was when the ancient Romans and Greeks were using it to cover their walls and floors—even creating mosaics that can still be seen and marveled at today.

The word *tile* covers several materials. However, in general, when used alone, it refers to ceramic tile. There are also stone tiles—including marble and cement—and ceramic tiles made to resemble various stones.

Textured stone, such as limestone, tumbled marble and slate, is generally

▼ For this floor, the look of marble is accomplished through porcelain stone. This line of stone comes in 10 colors that can have a polished or unpolished finish.

▶ Since it's often the place where you start your day, the bath should be inviting and fun. Creative design elements, like tiles formed into a "rug," are a great way to introduce a little energy into this very personal space.

considered nonslip. If you are considering stone for your floor, bear in mind that unsealed stone will stain. Have the surface professionally sealed with a natural finish when it is installed and each year thereafter. Stone is susceptible to scratching and chipping, but these tiny defects can add to the patina and the rustic charm of the floor.

When shopping for floor tiles, you'll find the same two basic categories used for wall tiles: glazed and unglazed. Both types are made of fired clay that is molded either by hand or machine into an unbelievable range of shapes,

sizes and textures. Glazed tile, which is impervious to water and stains and is quite hard, is the best choice for a bath. Grout lines can darken or stain if not properly sealed, so be sure your tile installer is experienced. Also consider choosing a dark grout, as opposed to the standard white.

Metallic tiles are as popular for bathroom floors as they are for walls. Some metallic tiles are actually ceramic tiles that have a metallic finish added after firing. Others are tiles that have the metallic surface applied to a phenolic resin or cement backing.

▼ The warm color of these porcelain tiles combined with an inlaid mosaic border bring a hint of Italian villas to this soothing bathroom.

▲ The luxurious look in this bath comes from marble tiles paired with a mosaic border.

Croc Rocks

From boots to belts, crocodile prints add a splash of the exotic to fashion. Now, croc is available in the home, where you can adorn your floors with the colors and textures of this intriguing animal skin. The textural, rich flooring creates a chic setting, and because it's vinyl, it's a great, low-maintenance choice for the bath. Furthermore, the product resists tears, rips and gouges, and it's softer underfoot than wood floors.

▲ This sunken whirlpool tub, walls and floor are all done in glass mosaic tile, available in more than 60 colors.

▲ Today's baths are no longer simply utilitarian. These deco tiles transform a floor from fine to fabulous.

◀ This above-counter basin is crafted of bronze, a finish that will evolve over time to gain a rich patina.

fabulous fixtures

▲ This faucet's polished brass lends glamour to an otherwise simple form and adds an element of the unexpected to a minimalist, contemporary bath.

Creating a bath that meets every one of your family's needs depends on a variety of factors, starting with a layout that works. Probably the most fun part of the planning process, though, is selecting fittings and fixtures that suit your style and your lifestyle. After all, here's where you get to add all those pretty amenities you've been dreaming of—an oversize whirlpool tub, a steam shower for two, pedestal sinks and more. But with so many bath fixtures to choose from, it helps to know what you're looking for before you head to the showroom or home center.

When selecting counters and sinks, for example, you'll need to decide how you would like the sink basin to sit—either above the counter or below. Will you be installing a tub or just a stall shower? What type of toilet will fit best in your space? Perhaps there's even room for a bidet. Maybe you'd like to include some *real* luxuries. A dual-sink vanity gives partners valuable extra elbowroom, and a separate toilet compartment allows for more privacy. Everything down to the smallest detail is important: Faucet handles and cabinet and door hardware that feels wonderful in your hand will delight you every day. To make shopping for fixtures easier, arm yourself with all the information you'll need to make the best choices for you.

sinks

▲ Form and function are one in this lavatory. Its nonporous surface repels bacteria, contributing to a more sanitary bathroom.

Today's sinks can be truly artistic. With beautiful proportions, rich colors and decorative finishes, these sculptural forms can make your bath extraordinary. And whether you like a minimalist look or one that's infused with tradition, you're sure to find the perfect fixture and fittings.

There are six basic sink styles on the market today. The style you choose will depend on your taste, budget and the size of your space. Self-rimming sinks are installed in an opening in the countertop. Adhesive applied to the raised rim or lip, which rests on top of the counter, holds the sink in place and forms a waterproof seal. Under-mount basins are joined to the vanity surface from below, so there is no raised lip—a boon for easy cleanup. Integral sinks are perhaps the most hygienic option. Manufactured from solid surfacing, they are fused with the countertop to form one seamless, easily maintained unit. Vessel sinks usually rest above the counter, allowing their shapes and

STYLE NOTES

Clean Finish

Toto has introduced an innovative new finish called SanaGloss. The finish, which can be found on select lavatories and toilets, helps prevent staining and reduces the growth of mold and bacteria. With SanaGloss, vitreous porcelain requires the barest maintenance—only an occasional wipe with a damp sponge or cloth.

▲ Outfitting the bath with coordinated fixtures lends a pulled-together look for high-end style.

▲ Stainless steel is as at home in the bath as it is in the kitchen. This hammered stainless-steel sink lends immediate artistic impact, making it a great choice for a main-floor powder room.

▲ This washbasin is made of solid Bihara stone, perfect for a natural-looking, minimalist room.

colors to function almost as sculpture within the room. Vessels are made of everything from fireclay, stone or metal to heavy-duty glass. Pedestal sinks have a classic, traditional look. Keep in mind, however, that pedestals offer no storage underneath and little surface area for toiletries. Console sinks, which stand on two or four legs rather than on a central pedestal, provide wide, practical decks, but like pedestals, they offer no storage.

When shopping for a sink, you'll also find a wide range of options in materials, including vitreous china, marble and other stones, solid surfacing and stainless steel. Composites, or cultured stone, are made of granite or quartz particles suspended in a polyester resin. Fireclay, a durable ceramic, offers a hard, glossy finish and is strong enough to sustain larger designs, some of which almost resemble furniture. And other materials, like glass, hammered metal, concrete, wood and stone, have taken vessel sinks to new heights of style. Just keep in mind that these products are most appropriate for a powder room, where they'll receive less wear and tear.

▲ Compact yet eye-catching, this pedestal can fit almost anywhere. The clever design includes a space-saving built-in towel rack.

▼ Pipes might not be the first thing you think of when choosing a glass sink, but they are an important consideration. Because the plumbing is exposed, each component must gleam like the faucet you chose so carefully.

▲ This sink brings a new level of minimalist tranquility to the bath.

▲ This handcrafted wrought-iron base with an above-counter basin has a Spanish influence from an earlier era.

▲ This lavatory pairs a golden finish with a classic under-counter sink for a modern look.

◀ Inspired by decorative ceramics of past eras, this basin captures the ample proportions of the classic washbasin and brings to it the conveniences of modern technology.

▲ This self-rimming porcelain sink features carved moldings that frame the basin.

▲ This dramatic double console, available in more than 20 shades of transparent or sandblasted lacquered glass, is coupled with handmade oval ceramic basins.

▲ This above-counter basin cleverly mimics the look of ice-encrusted glass.

▲ Traditional but not fussy, this self-rimming sink features subtle flourishes like a gently raised lip and octagonal shape.

STYLE NOTES

Starck Difference

Philippe Starck, the world-renowned industrial designer known for his sleek interiors in such hotels as the Royalton in New York City and the Delano in South Beach, Florida, is currently focusing his attention on the bath. His new collection includes a variety of sinks, toilets and shower trays all with the designer's signature minimalist style. Perfect for residential use, the Jelly-Cube sink shown above features a square basin mounted on a translucent acrylic cube and simple metal legs. The modestly sized unit, which comes with or without the backsplash, will fit into almost any space—and the two bottom drawers allow just enough room for items like toiletries and extra hand towels to be neatly stowed away.

▲ Why not opt for an unexpected element in the bath? The eye-catching texture of a hammered metal sink adds instant impact.

▲ This pedestal sink, with cut corners and an angled base, is 30 inches wide to allow for plenty of surface space and elbowroom.

▲ This sink is based on the look of classic Grecian fountains, but boasts all the practicality of traditional modern sinks. It's available in a range of basin and mosaic combinations.

▶ This pedestal and bowl has a clean, minimalist design. The pedestal is finished in chrome. The vessel, molded from solid surfacing, is available in several solid colors.

▲ Pedestal sinks aren't only for super-size master suites and pocket-size powder rooms. A modest pedestal can give even a midsize bathroom an air of elegance.

▲ This glass-top sink with an integral bowl of frosted glass is designed with small baths and powder rooms in mind.

▼ For a totally stunning look, a basin of red-toned glass is set atop a water-texture glass counter with bronze-plated sculpted legs.

▲ This sleek and sophisticated wall-mounted lavatory set lends modern appeal to the bath.

▲ Make your bath sparkle with a wide-spread faucet in chrome.

Like a work of art, a new faucet can add a bit of whimsy, set a tone or even act as a central design focus in your bathroom. The range of styles and material choices has transformed these once strictly utilitarian details into architectural centerpieces. For purely dressing up the sink or adding finishing touches to the bath without exorbitant cost, nothing compares with some of the newest designs in faucets. And many of the choices offer surprising functionality.

Embellish the charm of a turn-of-the-century bath with Victorian faucets, which include scrolled knobs and a pewter finish to complement a clawfoot tub and pedestal sink. For more contemporary tastes, use faucet sets that have free-flowing shapes and colored ceramic finishes. You'll find dozens of options with simple yet strong lines and sensuous detailing. Of course, the standards are still available—cross-handle knobs, levers, ball handles and simple straight spouts.

What you'll discover, though, is that most of these time-honored designs have been given updated details for a fresher, more unique look.

Some faucets have also been given an upgrade in the technology department and include sensors that detect changes in pressure and temperature when water is being turned on at another faucet in the house. These marvels automatically adjust pressure and temperature to keep them more constant. Some even have anti-scald features.

▲ This stylish single-handle faucet is easy to operate.

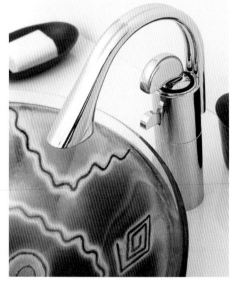

▲ A single-handle faucet in chrome lends a distinctly modern look when paired with an above-counter glass basin.

▲ For a new twist on a sophisticated chrome cross-handle faucet set, try a wall-mounted version.

Fittings

The different types of faucets available for the bathroom can be distinguished by the way the unit's handles and spouts are arranged.

Two-handle faucets are most commonly used in the bath. They feature a single base unit that holds the spout and both hot and cold valves. Lately, though, single-handle faucets have also been gaining popularity in the bath. They include a center-set knob or lever above the spout, which makes them very easy to use. Wide-spread faucets have hot and cold valves and spouts that are all mounted separately. They work well for wall-mounted applications or for hard-to-fit high-design sinks and tubs.

When shopping for faucets, you'll need to know about "centers"—the distance between the center of one handle and the center of the other. Lavatory faucets mounted on the basin usually have 4-inch centers but can come in 6 or 8 inches. Wall-mounted lavatory faucets can come in 4½-inch and 6-inch centers. If you are replacing an old faucet, the easiest thing to do is take it with you to purchase a new one.

Form & Finish

Faucets are typically formed of either metal or plastic at their bases. The best quality and longest-lasting faucets are made from solid brass. Of course, this is also the most expensive option. Faucets made with zinc-alloy bodies are a good compromise. They're durable and less costly than brass. Plastic varieties, on the other hand, are inexpensive but do not perform as well as the metal types.

As for faucet finishes, they vary from the standard chrome and brass to pewter and nickel. There are also com-

▼ This faucet, which is available in a wall-mounted, single-hole tap, is a pretty choice when only cold water is needed.

binations of finishes, such as chrome and nickel. Higher-end faucets include bisque and ceramic finishes and fine metal overlays of gold or sterling silver for detailing.

You will also have plenty of color options—even for faucets with a metallic finish. You'll find everything from classic polished or satin chrome and brass to brushed copper and nickel with deep bronze and warm silvery tones. Selecting a painted or enameled finish will really allow you to coordinate your faucets with the rest of your bath design scheme.

▲ Create a distinctive bath by combining deck-mounted and wall-mounted faucets in satin nickel.

▲ This faucet has Italian styling that works particularly well for above-counter sinks. It is available in chrome, satin, brass and blacksmith finishes.

▲ This electronic faucet provides automatic off/on activation and convenient temperature control. The handles are available in six interchangeable color options.

◀ If you'd like to add a bit of drama to your bath, you'll love the cosmopolitan look of this faucet.

▲ A rubbed-oil bronze finish gives this faucet a rich look.

Smart Filter

Now you can get the great taste of filtered water right from the tap with the AquaSuite PureTouch faucet from Moen. The filter, which has been approved by the American Dental Association, does not filter out all-important fluoride.

▲ For a classic look that has modern solid-brass construction, consider a wide-spread faucet like this one. It's available in a variety of finishes.

showers

details, details, details

▲ The curved shape of this 6-foot shower eliminates the need for a shower door, creating an open effect. The mirrored back wall completes the luxurious picture.

Perhaps the area of the bathroom that has seen the most innovation in recent years is the shower. It has gone from a simple soap-and-shampoo spot to an authentic at-home spa. No matter what you want from your shower, chances are there is a manufacturer out there that has exactly what you want—or can make it for you.

Many showers are prefabricated, but they can also be custom designed and built on-site. Custom showers are framed like walls and finished with a variety of materials, including ceramic tile, glass block and marble. Another common feature on these units is walls and doors made of safety glass. Some manufacturers are now offering trackless glass doors, which are easier to clean and offer a more open look.

Prefabricated units, which are less expensive than custom-made models, are usually manufactured of molded plastics like acrylic or fiberglass. They are available in a wide range of colors, shapes and sizes.

Whether you choose a custom or prefabricated shower, you'll find a wide range of accessories available, including multiple massaging showerheads, an adjustable handheld sprayer mounted on a sliding bar, a seat, overhead lighting, a mirror and even sound systems with AM/FM radios and CD players. Some "smart" faucets can even be preprogrammed to control both the temperature and the volume of the water flow. There are so many options available today in showerheads

▲ Pamper every inch of your body with a multihead shower system.

▲ This classically designed showerhead has more than 75 jets to produce a 9-inch spray of water.

▲ Tranquility is key in this grotto-like bath. A large showerhead provides a soothing cascade while individual jets and a handheld massager head relax tired muscles.

that these fixtures make up a category unto themselves. Satisfying the demand for more luxurious baths, manufacturers have heeded the call for showers that offer multiple nozzles and massaging sprayers with differing spray options. Now one head can bathe you in a rainlike shower while another massages your lower back. There are also showerheads that slide on a pole to different heights to accommodate all users. And a new option on some showerheads allows the head itself to be pivoted a full 360 degrees for the ultimate in positioning.

Spa Style

No longer a passing dream, the idea of spa-style showers in the home has been made a reality by savvy manufacturers in tune with the lifestyle demands of homeowners. Everything from lavish, complete shower systems to easy-to-install and maintain massaging showerheads are now available.

If you're looking for true spalike quality, you'll want to consider one of the many high-end shower systems. The most complete include an enclosure of tempered glass and/or acrylic with designer colors and patterns and a

variety of complementary trim choices. Coordinating faucets and other fixtures adds a stylish touch. These relaxing spa showers feature various combinations of sprays and nozzles that soothe, relax, invigorate and drench, according to your whim. Most have at least one standard showerhead, a handheld sprayer and two to four body sprays or massage jets. The standard showerheads are often directionally adjustable or may telescope for exact placement of spray.

Both stationary and handheld sprayers offer adjustments for intensity

▼ Artfully styled, this handshower reinvents English craftsmanship through scale, proportion and detail.

High-Style Shower

For the ultimate stall shower, experts suggest installing one that will accommodate two people—when space permits. Add a ceiling-mounted rainhead fixture for a cloudburst-like soaking. Finally, a frameless glass shower door will really open up your space. A stall shower with this kind of unobtrusive-looking door works in any style of bath.

▲ An update to a classic, the brushed brass finish on this shower collection offers a subtle, sophisticated look.

▲ Made of Lucite acrylic, this shower system is watertight and easy to clean.

▲ Customized to your preference, many shower systems offer a range of showerheads, handles, body sprays and jets to make every shower experience feel like a day at the spa.

and type of spray. The body sprays on some are mounted on vertical runs that allow them to slide up or down as you choose. Thermostatically controlled water mixers maintain constant water temperature and pressure. Many of these complete shower systems also include storage ledges and may even have built-in seats.

If you don't have thousands to spend on a new shower or aren't looking to remodel your shower area, don't despair. You can still get spa-shower relaxation. If you have a shower enclosure that you want to transform into a spa-type shower, units are available that feature many of the same pampering elements as the complete shower systems. Some of the more innovative of these midrange options are completely housed units that are easy to install. Others allow you to customize your options by choosing from a menu of sprayers, showerheads and handles that are each separately installed in the shower.

You can also include a steam unit in an existing shower. Most have automatic time and temperature selections. In some, you can also introduce aromatherapy options to the steam for a more relaxing vapor. The bottom line is that the luxury of a spa-type shower can be realized by just about everyone regardless of the amount you have to spend. Naturally, the more elaborate and customized the unit, the higher the price, but the simplest massaging showerheads that fit right onto existing plumbing connections are usually under $100.

If you don't want to invest large sums until you've tried out the joy of jetted shower sprays, consider massaging showerheads. Perfect for meager budgets, these can be installed by even a novice home plumber. Simply trade out a regular showerhead for one of these models. Manufacturers offer a good selection of styles to complement your existing fixtures and bath decor.

▲ Take control of your shower with a handshower. Unique technology allows the user to freely position water flow.

▲ This shower features an ergonomic handle, a pressure-balanced valve to prevent scalding and a three-way adjustable showerhead.

▶ For the ultimate in showering sleekness, consider a shower without a door. The unique curved design of this unit keeps the spray inside.

◀ Customize your basic shower/tub combination with pretty glass doors and tile accents for the bath alcove.

▲ Streamline your shower with decorative urethane moldings that resist moisture.

▼ Cool and compact, this shower unit fits virtually anywhere and includes recessed halogen lights and more than 100 spray channels.

Let Off Some Steam

When is a shower more like a vacation? When you add a little steam to the equation. The moist warmth of a steam bath helps
relieve muscle tension, cleanse skin impurities and reduce stress. Now you can achieve the rejuvenating benefits of a good steam right in your own home with this freestanding steam bath and shower combination. Constructed of high-quality sanitary acrylic, this unit offers plenty of space for two.

▲ Both showerheads on this all-in-one shower system can be rotated 360 degrees. Mounted on a tubular arm that pivots 180 degrees, they can also be rotated for use as body sprays.

▲ This frameless bath enclosure system offers durable, watertight construction in a variety of sizes and heights. Its magnetic latch gives the door an especially solid feel.

▲ A large shower with a built-in seat and multiple showerheads is the ultimate in luxury.

▲ This shower system offers a cylindrical showerhead, dual-spray handshower, body sprays and a concealed shampoo tray.

◀ A single plumbing connection for this shower system allows for seven water ports, two telescopic shower arms, four body sprays and a personal handshower.

▲ These 8-foot-tall waterproof panels can be installed over existing shower walls. They are made of solid-surface materials and can be cut to fit almost any shower dimension.

▲ Nothing brings the spa experience into your home like a roomy shower stall, complete with wood floor, multiple showerheads and a heated towel rack.

▲ This freestanding acrylic tub offers stylish luxury with a convenient built-in towel bar.

A bathtub is an essential element and probably the fixture people think of first when they imagine a luxurious bathroom. As life gets more and more complicated, we yearn to have time for ourselves and a place where we can relax. Today, many people are rediscovering the restorative power of lounging in a tub filled with a soothing fragrance. And even if you personally prefer showers, it makes sense to include a tub in your plans—if only for resale appeal.

When selecting a tub, make sure it will fit in the space properly, allowing enough room for other fixtures and basic bathroom traffic. Options range from 5-foot-long remodeler tubs designed to fit into an existing tub recess to luxurious freestanding claw-foot models. An average-size tub is 32 by 60 inches, but much larger models are available. Some manufacturers produce all-in-one units, which are usually acrylic and offer a tub and shower surround in a single piece.

The highest-quality tubs are made of enameled cast iron. But if you want an oversize tub, consider a fiberglass-reinforced acrylic model. These are lightweight—so you may not have to reinforce the floor—and can be molded into comfortable forms, with built-in armrests, headrests and grab bars.

For the ultimate in luxury, opt for a soaking tub. These circular tubs, generally 29 to 32 inches high, take less time to fill than a whirlpool and don't require an integral heater.

▲ An overflowing bath provides near total immersion for the ultimate in relaxation.

▲ Doubling as a work of art, this tub is an extra-deep vessel made of DuPont Corian.

▲ This soaking tub is inspired by designs of the late 1800s.

Finding the Right Tub

If you're on a budget, you may want to opt for a standard-size tub made of porcelain-coated steel. Bear in mind, though, that this type is thinner and more prone to chipping than those crafted from other materials, and bathwater may cool more rapidly in this type of tub because steel conducts heat.

Tubs made of acrylic, which can be molded into any number of shapes, start at about $350. These offer design flexibility and are lightweight and very durable. Acrylic tubs resist chipping, provide good insulation and retain heat for longer periods of time than steel tubs do. Some acrylic models also incorporate special features for safety and comfort, such as grab bars and lumbar supports.

If you're willing to pay for a bit of luxury, enamel-coated cast-iron tubs offer elegance and durability. Although prices start at about $400, expect to pay closer to $1,500 for a luxury model, such as a slipper-style tub with hand-painted details and claw-foot legs. Cast-iron tubs are more durable than steel because they have a stronger metal and thicker finish. Like steel, however, cast iron tends to be cold and draws heat away from the water. One last caveat: Some weigh in at more than 500 pounds without water, so be sure your floor can hold the weight. Often, homeowners will need to add reinforcement to floor joists to accommodate the burden.

For the same look and cost of cast iron at half the weight, try a tub made of composite materials. Combining the style and durability of cast iron in a lighter material, these tubs are easier to install and warmer to the touch than their cast-iron counterparts.

▼ This whirlpool tub, which features a gold rim, is designed to be mounted under granite, marble or tile.

Squeaky Clean

Whichever model you choose, take care to avoid cleaning your tub with harsh solvents and scouring pads, which could scratch or dull the finish. Instead, choose nonabrasive cleansers applied with soft cloths or sponges to protect and preserve the fixture.

▲ Add an extra touch of luxury to your bath with a handheld shower.

▲ This soaking tub was handcrafted in England in a luxurious vintage style.

▲ This octagonal whirlpool bath measures a luxurious 72 inches by 48 inches.

▲ The organic shape of this oval tub has a carefully carved edge that provides a comfortable headrest. Three different types of individually adjustable jets give a custom massage.

Whirlpools

In the past 10 years, whirlpool tubs have gone from being the ultimate symbol of bathroom opulence to a standard piece of master suite equipment. And there have never been so many options to choose from.

Top-of-the-line whirlpools are made of enameled cast iron and hold a high-gloss finish indefinitely. However, acrylics are equally popular, since they maintain water temperature better than cast iron, are lightweight and can be molded into a range of shapes.

Remodeler units fit right into a standard tub recess. If you want to splurge, larger deluxe models can accommodate two or more people and offer intensive massage options.

You might also consider enhancing your whirlpool bath by purchasing accessories like an integral heater to maintain the desired water temperature throughout your soak, a cascading faucet and a handheld sprayer. For a true spalike experience, you'll want to choose a tub with adjustable jets. Look for a jet system that allows you to

change the direction of water flow and the air-to-water ratio. More air means a stronger massage, whereas more water creates a gentler effect. Some new whirlpools work by forcing air alone through the jets, so bathwater isn't recirculated through the system.

Whichever type you choose, it's a good idea to talk to your architect or contractor before you purchase a whirlpool tub. He or she may recommend that you purchase an additional hot-water heater and/or reinforce your bathroom floor prior to installation.

▲ This whirlpool bath combines artistry and technology in a distinctive pedestal tub that accommodates a 10-inch flat-screen TV, DVD and CD stereo system. Built for two, it even has a floating remote control.

Get Soaked

A decadent alternative to a whirlpool tub, soaking—or bathing—tubs don't have jets and motors. Considered easier to maintain than whirlpools, soaking tubs allow bathers to add bubbles, salts and aromatherapy oils to the water. Such therapeutic potions could clog or damage the jets of a whirlpool tub. Soaking tubs come in hundreds of shapes, sizes and colors, as well as a host of materials, so let your personal preference and budget serve as your guide.

▲ With its ergonomic loungers and built-in television, CD player, stereo and speakers, this whirlpool tub is more gathering spot than tub!

This toilet is crafted from high-fired vitreous china with a triple-glazed glossy finish.

▼ Your toilet may be utilitarian, but it doesn't have to look that way. This stainless steel and wood toilet is anything but simple.

Once a necessity, now a design statement, the humble toilet has come a long way. Most of today's models are made of beautiful yet durable vitreous china, a long-lasting and stain-resistant material, and offer much in the way of styling and performance. In fact, the latest toilet units consume far less water than their predecessors did. To comply with the Comprehensive Energy Policy Act, a federal law that was enacted to conserve energy, toilets manufactured within the United States must now use no more than 1.6 gallons of water per flush. That's an estimated savings for a family of four of more than 10,000 gallons of water per year. Another feature you'll want to be sure to ask the dealer about: Today's toilets often include flushing mechanisms that are less noisy than older models. And the innovations don't end there. Some manufactures now offer a line of remote-control, heated toilet seats and personal sanitizers.

Form & Function

When shopping around for a toilet you will find that, in general, they function in one of two ways: gravity flush and pressurized flush.

Gravity flush is the most common type of toilet. In this system, a tank is supported by and bolted onto a separate bowl. Water from the tank enters the bowl via openings circling the rim. Gravity-fed pressure then forces the water and waste out of the bowl. With a pressurized flush, compressed air

Try "One" on for Size

For a sleek, sophisticated look, consider a one-piece toilet. These model types combine the tank and bowl in a single unit, so they can be easier to clean. Also called low-profile toilets, these models often include elongated bowls. The longer bowl tends to stay cleaner than the smaller type because it has a larger water surface.

▲ Clean styling and advanced, quick-refill flushing make this one-piece toilet a welcome addition to any bathroom.

▲ As elegant as it is simple, this toilet is a real space saver.

▶ Attach the Jasmin washlet seat to your toilet for the ultimate in luxury, as well as hygiene.

from a sealed chamber inside the tank forces water into and through the bowl. This type of mechanism is used in one-piece toilets because the tank on these models is often not high enough to create sufficient gravity-fed pressure. The downside to this system is that some units can be noisy.

Measuring Up

If you are replacing a toilet, rather than starting from scratch, you'll want to make sure your new toilet will fit properly in the vacated space. You don't want to pay a plumber to move pipes if you don't absolutely have to. You need to measure the existing rough-in, which is the distance from the center of the floor drain to the surface of the wall, before you select your new toilet. Most toilets have a 12-inch rough-in dimension, but some, particularly those in older houses, measure 10 or 14 inches.

Also keep in mind that if you are replacing a toilet that consumes more than 1.6 gallons of water per flush, you may need to hire a plumber to move the drain to accommodate one of today's low-flush models.

▲ This one-piece toilet has contoured details and a low profile, plus the powerful gravity flushing mechanism.

◀ This regal decorated toilet features a metallic gold design.

No longer the "forgotten" fourth bathroom fixture, bidets can add more than functionality to the bath—as this piece with its elegant chrome and brass fixtures shows.

▲ This toilet is made of heavy-gauge stainless steel and features an elongated bowl.

▲ This commode—more like furniture than a toilet—is fit for a king.

▲ This one-piece toilet benefits from a powerful siphon-jet flush action.

◀ Could your master bath use a little drama? Fixed windows, like the trapezoids shown here, are one way to add instant flair. And you'll brighten the space in the process.

the well-lit bath

▲ These unique resin sconces work beautifully with just about any decor, whether traditional or modern.

Illumination holds the key to unlocking the potential of any room in the house—and the bath is no exception. New-home builders and homeowners state categorically that the one place they want to fill with amenities for relaxation is the bath. So it's the perfect room to treat with the ideal windows or decorative lighting fixtures to help set a serene mood.

There are many ways to create the perfectly lit place of repose in your bath. If given the choice, most people would choose to flood the bath with natural light. And though privacy is a concern in this room, there's no reason lots of windows can't work. After all, natural light provides the best milieu for applying makeup by allowing more normal skin tones and creating fewer shadows and glare than artificial light. Transoms over the lavatory area and over a soaking tub let in soft, natural light without compromising your privacy. Skylights and solar tubes bring in an even greater amount of light.

Of course, no matter how sun-filled and private your room is, no bath would be complete—or practical—without lighting fixtures. Whatever your needs, whether it's bright lighting for over the mirror or delicate sconces for adding ambiance, there's a fixture that's perfect for you. With so many styles to choose from, there's a light for every bathroom look.

▲ When you're designing your ideal bathroom, chances are your plan will include lots of sunshine. Consider planning a windowed bay for the tub area—you'll enjoy those relaxing soaks even more by sunlight or starlight.

Windows can transform a room like no other amenity. Smaller rooms, such as the bath, are opened up dramatically with the right windows, yet retain their warmth and intimacy. Windows add views, natural light and architectural integrity, and they also serve as a primary means of ventilating and cooling. If planned well, windows and coverings will allow you to take the best advantage of outside breezes, setting up airflow patterns that keep the airspace in your bathroom fresh.

Window Types

Because windows make up a significant portion of any building budget, their careful selection is tantamount to a successful project. So before you settle on just any double-hung window, brush up on the options available.

Double-hung or tilt windows have two sashes that move up and down, one behind the other. Only half the window area can be opened, either the top, the bottom or a little of both. These versatile windows can be found in country and traditional homes, as well as in some contemporaries. They function well and have minimal space requirements, so they work well behind furniture and in corners.

Single-hung windows are the same as the double-hung units except the top sash doesn't move.

Sliding windows have two or more panels that cross each other when they open, like a double-hung set on its side. They are unobtrusive and easy to open, close and clean.

Casement windows are hinged on one side and are operated with a crank. Look for multipoint locking, especially on tall ones, for both safety and a tight seal. You also might want to consider special "egress" hardware that opens the windows wide enough for emergency exiting.

Awning windows are like casements turned sideways. They're hinged at the top, and the crank turns the bottom out. This allows fresh air in but still keeps out the rain. Awning windows

▲ Lots of windows and a skylight are welcome additions to any bath. Relax under the stars while soaking at night and enjoy a sun-filled bathroom during the day.

▲ Acrylic block panels allow natural light into the bathroom without sacrificing privacy. They are precaulked, sealed to prevent condensation and treated with an antifungicide.

are typically used in combination with a fixed window.

Fixed windows, also known as direct sets, don't open at all. An example of this can commonly be found in a bay window where the center part might be fixed. Fixed windows come in all sizes and shapes, including parallelograms, triangles, octagons and trapezoids. You can even design your own shape.

Bow windows are multiple windows that curve gradually rather than forming angles. Bay windows are a combination of three or more windows that angle out from the house. The center unit is parallel to the house, while the side units sit at an angle. If the bay is formed with right angles, it is called a box bay. A small box bay with a glass top, often used in the kitchen, is called a garden bay.

Skylights and solar tubes are particularly popular for baths. They allow natural light to enter the room through the roof, thereby taking up no wall space and permitting privacy. Skylights are just like windows except they install in the roof. They are most often fixed, though some companies offer versions that are operable to admit fresh air. Solar tubes use a system of highly reflective tubes from the roof to an interior area. They are easy to install and can go places that even skylights won't work.

Material Matters

The frame—the fixed section of the window that holds the glass panes and hardware—plays an important role in how a unit looks and functions. Frames can be constructed from a variety of materials, including solid wood, vinyl, aluminum and various combinations of two or more components.

▼ Arched windows are among the geometric shapes that can make your home distinctive—inside and out. Casement windows flank the center window in this bath and each has divided lights for traditional appeal.

▲ Bay and bow windows are used in combination to capture a panoramic view outside this master bathroom.

Wood is strong, and for that reason it has been the most common framing material for centuries. It is still a popular choice because of its availability, the ease with which it can be milled into custom shapes and designs and because it can be easily painted or stained to the homeowner's whim. Most important, it's the best insulator against outside elements. There is a downside to wood, however. Wood windows require regular maintenance because they are susceptible to expansion and rot when exposed to moisture. As a result, they must be regularly sealed with paint or

▲ These simple windows are the perfect frames for the dramatic scenery right outside.

Made in the Shade

Beautiful large windows turn a room into a sun-drenched retreat, but all that openness can be tricky in the bathroom. For the best of both worlds, look for shades that have a top-down and bottom-up feature. You can pull the shades up to expose the bottom part of the window or pull them down to let the light in through the top part of the window.

▲ These casement windows feature a decorative flexi-frame accent with custom grilles for a dramatic look.

▲ The classic look of double-hung windows allows plenty of light into the bath while maintaining a traditional focus.

Aluminum frames are strong, lightweight and come in a wide selection of shapes. They are available in a number of anodized, or baked-on, enamel finishes, which makes them quite durable and easy to maintain. Right now, the big drawback of aluminum windows is that they insulate poorly and allow heat loss and condensation. Advances are being made to address this problem, however, so that is something to look out for. Better-quality aluminum windows are equipped with thermal breaks—a less conductive material, like plastic—that separate the interior and exterior surfaces of the window, allowing better climate control. Price-wise, aluminum-framed windows compare to high-quality vinyl frames.

A window frame that is composed of two or more materials, called a composite, draws on the individual strengths of each material. For example, vinyl-clad wood windows combine the strength of wood with the durability and weather resistance of vinyl. Specifically, the inside surfaces of the window are made of wood so they can be painted or stained. The outside surface is made from vinyl for ease of maintenance.

Aluminum-clad wood windows are made of wood on the interior and aluminum on the exterior, making them more climate impervious. Aluminum-clad wood is strong, durable and available in a range of sizes and colors, like vinyl, but may not be appropriate for a new home with a historical design.

stained for protection. However, a well-built, well-maintained wood window could last hundreds of years. The price tag for unfinished wood windows is 15 to 40 percent more than for vinyl.

Vinyl frames are a popular choice for residential windows because they insulate well, stand up to the elements and require little maintenance. They are inexpensive and durable, and unlike wood, vinyl frames resist moisture. Vinyl frames do not require painting and are available in a number of color options. And, the color goes all the way through the frame, so dings and scratches are hard to see. Early vinyl windows had problems with thermal expansion, resulting in windows that fit poorly, leaked or cracked, but recent advances have improved their stability. In terms of cost, vinyl can be relatively inexpensive, although prices vary according to the thickness of the material and the assembly technique involved. The only downside to vinyl is that it is a relatively new material and therefore may not be well suited for historically inspired homes.

▲ This all-wood window includes a unique curved top. Because this home is in a secluded area, the homeowner was free to fill her wall space with windows.

Tech Check

Window technology continues to evolve, bringing us more attractive energy options.

• A new generation of low-E (low emissivity) coatings on windows will help lower your energy costs. Low-E technology not only keeps heat from escaping in winter but also blocks heat from coming into the home in summer. These types of products are referred to as solar control low-E or southern low-E windows.

• New technologies are mixing vinyl with wood in a formula that results in a strong, durable window available in a broader range of colors.

▲ A custom fixed, full-circle bathroom window with decorative muntins adds flair to a bath.

▲ A row of lights above the large vanity mirror coupled with two double-hung windows is the perfect combination for this grooming area.

In addition to allowing natural light to enter the bath, you'll also want to make artificial lighting a part of your design plan. Of course, good lighting in the bathroom is necessary for grooming. You have to be able to see yourself in the mirror when you're fixing your hair, applying makeup or shaving. But there is another very important consideration for bathroom lighting that most people don't think of: Good lighting can be essential to your feeling of well-being. If you look in the mirror and see someone with a healthy complexion looking back, you're ready to start the day. On the other hand, the wrong type of light can make you look and feel sickly even if you're feeling your best.

Artificial light should be ambient, and it should blend with the overall mood of the room. Recessed fixtures can unobtrusively delineate design features and produce soft pools of light throughout the bath or spa area. Fixtures placed on either side of the vanity, rather than on top, will shine a warm, flattering glow on the face, without creating shadows. Dimmer switches on all lights allow you to control the amount of illumination in the room by function and by area: brighter for dressing, softer for bathing. Finally, don't overlook candlelight as a source of illumination. Various types of candles, from pillars to votives, placed throughout the room create the perfect ambiance for quiet meditation or a soothing bath.

▲ Give your bath a refined touch with this uplight; the translucent shade casts a subtle glow.

▲ You don't need bright light above the tub, so a pendant is perfect here.

▲ This wall sconce is paired with a lens of hand-cut Baccarat crystal for glamour in the bathroom. The crystal is available in clear or cobalt blue, and the sconce comes in nickel silver, brushed nickel, chrome or sterling silver.

▶ Wall sconces finished in brushed nickel and topped with off-white shades add traditional charm to this bath.

▲ A true copy of a deco original, these hand-painted porcelain-bracket downlights—just 5 inches wide and 6 inches tall—replicate fixtures prevalent from the 1920s through the '50s.

STYLE NOTES

Fan-tastic

No doubt about it, the bathroom is the steamiest room in the house. Fogged mirrors are a minor irritation that's easily dealt with. Mildewed walls and peeling wallpaper, though, are bigger issues. The best solution is a bath fan. To determine how big a vent, or how many cubic feet per minute, you need for your bath, multiply the length and width of your bathroom by 1.1. You'll also want to take noise into consideration when shopping for your fan. The sound level of a vent is measured by an industry standard called a "sone." The level of one sone is about equal to the sound of a refrigerator.

▲ Suited for almost any style of home, this fixture was inspired by industrial spaces.

▲ This contemporary, elongated wall sconce provides an elegant focal point for the bath.

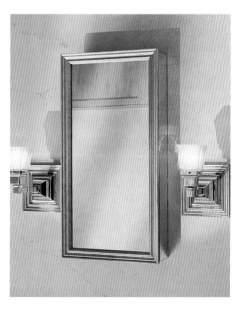

▲ The wood-frame mirrored cabinet and matching sconces make a perfect set.

MAKING IT HAPPEN

◀ There's no look more classic than a bathroom outfitted in crisp ceramic tile from head to toe. The secret is in combining sizes, shapes, colors and patterns for an effect that is at once fresh and inviting.

working with
professionals

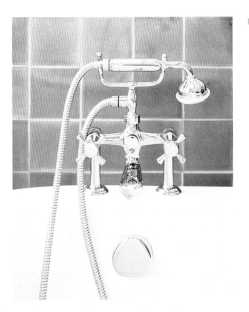

▲ This retro tub mixer with handshower sits on the rim of the tub for easy access.

The design/build team you hire is the key to the success of your project. The right team will not only guarantee satisfying results but will also ensure that the process is smooth and enjoyable. When planning your new bath, you will encounter a laundry list of professionals qualified to oversee the job. Which one is right for you depends on the scope and budget of your project.

Interview each member of your team thoroughly, making sure that he or she truly understands your project and your budget. Ask for and check several references. And don't forget about insurance: Each professional should be licensed and insured for worker's com-

pensation, as well as for property and personal liability. Always ask to see the insurance certificate of each person you hire. Also inquire about affiliations. Membership in a trade organization indicates professionalism.

No matter how well you plan, how carefully you choose your professionals or how airtight your contract may be, you'll have to be prepared to expect the unexpected from time to time. Seldom does any project proceed perfectly from start to finish. While you may not always be able to control circumstances, good communication with your contractor will keep you in the loop, despite the occasional bump in the road.

▲ One skill your designer should bring to the table is an eye for colors and how to mix and match them for the perfect effect.

An interior designer can play an important role in your project—from something as simple as helping you select colors and furnishings to a more complicated job like overseeing a team of professionals in a major remodel—but they are generally not qualified to plan structural redesigns. Because interior designers have access to manufacturers that sell only "to the trade," working with one can give you greater access to products and materials than you might have otherwise.

A certified bath designer (CBD) specializes in baths. For these professionals, all of whom are certified by the National Kitchen & Bath Association, comfort, safety and aesthetics are equal planning considerations in the success of your bath. CBDs attend trade shows and conferences to keep up-to-date on the latest products, materials and technologies, as well as on building and safety codes. They are experts in every area of bath design, from wiring, plumbing and ventilation to materials

and storage needs. If you decide to work with a CBD, you can expect a detailed outline of your project that describes every element to be included.

There are several ways CBDs can charge for their services. They may take a percentage of the entire job or charge a flat fee. Some charge an hourly fee or apply a markup to products ordered. Still others combine these two methods, charging an hourly rate of $50 to $100 and doubling the wholesale cost of goods.

▲ Everything works together in this bath. The Italian tiles behind the vanity are a perfect complement to the hand-painted mirror surrounds.

EXPERT TIP

Resources

For listings of qualified professionals in your area, contact these organizations:

• Architects—The American Institute of Architects (AIA) offers a national database of architects on its Web site, www.aia.org. You can also call your local chapter for referrals to professionals in your area.

• Interior designers—The American Society of Interior Designers (ASID) offers referrals, sample contracts and information. Call (800) 775-ASID or visit www.interiors.org.

• Contractors and remodelers—National Association of the Remodeling Industry (NARI); for referrals, call (800) 611-NARI, or visit www.nari.org.

• Certified Bath Designer—The National Kitchen & Bath Association (NKBA) has a wide range of bath design information on its Web site, www.nkba.com. For referrals, check the site or call (800) 843-6522.

▲ This glass sink, which was crafted by fusing layers of glass together, makes a dramatic design statement.

▲ Decorative touches like the silver shaving supplies add a bit of elegance—and free up storage space.

▶ The paneled tub mimics the custom cabinetry in this perfectly designed and executed bath.

▲ An architect will bring technical expertise—as well as an artistic eye—to your project.

If you're planning a comprehensive remodel or new construction job, an architect will probably be the first professional you contact to help plan the details of the project. Experts in structural, electrical and plumbing systems, architects are also artists who strive to bring beauty to every aspect of a space. By planning cost-efficient and functional spaces, skillfully negotiating bids with contractors and overseeing the project, an architect also may cut down your costs.

Architects deal with the entire scope of a project, from designing a space to ensuring that it is structurally sound to specifying materials and products for the contractor. Architects are also knowledgeable about building codes and zoning laws.

Generally, your architect will work with you to plan the new space, submitting several sets of drawings for your approval. The architect's final set of construction plans will give the contractor detailed specifications, from room dimensions to product placement. You can ask your architect to oversee construction—generally for a fee—but more often the architect's job will end with approval of the final plans, though he or she may help you find and hire a contractor.

An architect's fees can vary from an hourly rate to a fixed fee to a percentage of the total project cost—which is usually about 10 percent for small projects and between 7 and 10 percent for larger jobs.

Selecting Your Architect

Your preliminary interview with each architect you plan to consider can take place in your home or at his or her office, and it should last roughly one hour. During this meeting you should discuss your general ideas for the project—how much more space you need, what look you're going for, etc.—and ask the architect to explain the firm's design philosophy and its areas of expertise. Show the architect photos of building styles and even bathroom designs that you admire; the architect, in turn, will show you a portfolio of work the firm has completed.

Look for a common viewpoint and a rapport; you might be teamed with this person for six months or more. What kind of experience does he or she have in the style of design you prefer? Be up-front about your budget and ask for an explanation of the services the firm can provide and what their billing methods are: What do they charge to oversee construction? How many site visits would this generally entail? Charges might consist of a percentage of construction costs, a set fee, hourly rates, a sum per square foot built or a combination of these methods. Extra planning sessions may be billed hourly.

Before you commit to an architect, visit a couple of completed projects that the firm has worked on and check references. Once you have made your decision, work out a project timetable and put the terms of your agreement in writing. Standard contracts are available through the American Institute of Architects (AIA). Once you've signed on with an architect, you and that person become partners embarking on a mission together. The lines of communication should be open for perhaps the most stimulating part of the process—brainstorming and turning dreams into plans on paper.

▼ For this bath, the architect accommodated today's amenities in an old-fashioned setting, pairing a whirlpool tub with lead-glass windows and a custom-made shelf for toiletries.

▲ The architect who planned this bathroom saw this "bump out" as the perfect place for an oversize tub and plenty of windows.

The Process

According to the AIA, after hiring an architect there are generally six phases of a project.

1. Programming. This is when you discuss exactly what you want, what you need and what you can spend.

2. Presenting rough sketches. The architect provides a preliminary series of loosely drawn plans and perspectives. Until the details are finalized, costs may change.

3. Refining the design. Floor plans are drawn to scale and the architect lists the major materials and finishes.

4. Preparing construction documents. These are detailed drawings, usually in blueprint form, that include electrical plans and specifications.

5. Hiring a contractor. This can be someone you've heard about or someone your architect recommends. The contractor is responsible for construction methods, techniques, schedules and procedures.

6. Construction. Your architect will help guide the process of turning drawings into reality.

▲ An architect can help you make the most of your space, no matter how small. A corner shower unit is the perfect fit for a cozy bath.

▲ A clever extension of the tub surround and a small window occupy a corner of this bath that might otherwise have gone unused.

contractors

making it happen

▲ Working with a good contractor guarantees professional results—from the custom built-in tub platform to the simple moldings, every detail in this bathroom remodel is right on.

The general contractor (often called the GC or "the builder" in new construction projects) will execute the plans drawn up by your architect. Your contractor should also be familiar with local building codes and should procure all necessary permits—in fact, this responsibility should be outlined in your contract. Contractors also hire and supervise all tradespeople—who are called subcontractors—involved in the project, such as tile setters, plumbers and electricians. Your con-

tractor will coordinate work schedules and procedures and will be the person on-site to make sure the project is running smoothly.

Contractors' fees come in three different forms; make sure you know how the contractor will charge you before you accept a bid. Some work on a "cost-plus" basis. In other words, the contractor charges a fee for his or her services plus the cost of the project (materials, services of subcontractors, etc.). Others have a fixed fee—the best

option, since you know ahead of time what to expect. Still others work on a percentage of the total cost. If your contractor works on percentage, make sure you keep track of expenses throughout the project and ask your contractor for a cost breakdown before you pay the bill.

Most people seem to have dramatically different reactions to the building process. Some consider it to be one of the most rewarding experiences of their lives, while others, having tried it

▲ This integrated sink is molded with the counter in one piece of solid surfacing.

▲ A window with a sandblasted bottom half is a smart choice for the shower. Talk to your contractor about unique touches like this one before the project starts.

▲ From building a beadboard tub platform to installing the tile surround, your contractor must also be a craftsman.

once, never would do so again. The best way you can be certain that you'll fall into the first category is to make sure you've found a contractor who you can trust.

Getting Great Results

Every detail of the project—including plans, materials, schedule and payment structure—should be spelled out in a contract that is signed by both the client and the builder. Elements you'll need to specify range from the model and color of the bathroom sink you've selected to the style of the lighting fixtures you want over the vanity. In order to avoid conflict later, make your list of specifications as detailed as possible. (If you hire an architect to design the project, the makes and model numbers of all or most materials will probably be outlined in the blueprints. If not, you will most likely need to select them with your builder.)

Keep in mind, however, that no matter how detailed you try to be, some changes will inevitably arise. In such cases, you and the builder will need to sign a "change order," a document that serves as an amendment to the original written agreement, spelling out the alterations and who will be responsible for covering any additional costs. To keep construction on schedule and to avoid unnecessary expenses, be sure to make changes as early as possible. Halting or undoing work that has already been completed is costly and time consuming.

Finally, keep the lines of communication open. Keep a dialogue going with your contractor the whole time. Stay involved, visit the site, familiarize yourself with the process and if problems arise, address them quickly.

▼ The contractor on this project created a custom picture frame wainscot to lend an authentic vintage look to the bath.

▲ A skilled craftsman can turn your wall tile into a work of art.

▲ A contractor will be able to negotiate a better price on high-end items like these beautiful stone tiles for the shower.

▲ Ask your contractor about custom details like built-in wall shelves.

Questions for Your Contractor

Before you make a final commitment to working together, ask your contractor the following questions:

1. Does he or she specialize in high-end, mid-price or budget projects?

2. Does he or she have references from commercial banks and other lenders? A contractor in good financial standing will have no qualms about providing this information.

3. Does the contractor offer warranties on his or her work? Most will give a one-year warranty on the structure, but some offer up to 10 years.

4. Does he or she have client references?

5. How does he or she charge?

6. Will he or she submit competitive bids? Again, some in-demand contractors do not want to spend the time submitting bids if they know you are asking others to do the same. If one of your top choices is not willing to submit a competitive bid, you can ask just him or her to bid on the project and then negotiate, and possibly decline, if the bid comes in higher than you can afford.

7. What will be the day-to-day logistics of the project?

8. Once construction begins, how are changes to the plans to be handled?

9. Can you get a release-of-liens that shows all subcontractors have been paid? If you don't, a disgruntled worker may bill you after the contractor has moved on to the next project.

10. What about permits? Although laws vary from place to place, all new construction and most renovation projects require a building permit. The contractor should obtain the permit in his or her name. Don't work with a contractor who asks you to get the permit. To apply, your contractor will need to turn over the final blueprints so the building department can see what the project entails and issue the appropriate permit. This process can take two to six weeks.

▲ Have your contractor measure your doorways before you pick any large fixtures. An extra-deep soaking tub, for example, might not fit through the opening.

bids & contracts

▲ A marble floor and backsplash provide vintage charm but will increase your materials costs.

▲ Though it may be a bit more costly, a unique piece will set your bath apart.

Once you've determined the contractors you'd like to have bid on your project (approach at least three) you'll need to write a bid request. For the bids to be accurate and comparable, you must provide identical information to each bidder and be as detailed as possible. Include plans and a list of all materials, fixtures and fittings with brand names, model numbers and colors. Then set a deadline for all bids to be in—one to three weeks is reasonable.

All bids should be professionally presented, typewritten on company letterhead and signed by the professional. Each one should include the following:
• A price for materials and labor. Labor must be included, otherwise you may find yourself paying much more than expected. Beware of a "time-and-materials" arrangement; these give the contractor no incentive to finish the job, exposing you to extra expense.
• Fees for demolition, rebuilding, debris removal and cleaning.

• A price for all products. Double-check your materials list so nothing is overlooked.
• A statement, in writing, specifying how long the bid will be effective. If the contractor will honor the bid for only one week, you'll be out of luck if your other bids don't come in for two.

Keep in mind that the cost of obtaining all necessary permits, inspections, licenses and insurance is the contractor's responsibility. This should be detailed in the bid. The bid should also

▲ The owners of this bathroom planned for a lot of storage space.

▲ Mix inexpensive decorating details, like a pretty soap dish or a sheaf of sea grass, with more costly fixtures to stretch your budget dollars.

state any work that will not be completed by the contractor, such as disposing of old fixtures. It's often a wise idea to ask your architect or designer to look over each bid.

If you've provided each of the contractors with an identical bid request, the proposals should not vary by more than 5 to 10 percent. Be wary of any bid that comes in exceptionally low or high, and ask to meet with the contractor to go over the proposal together. If you're examining a low bid, tell the contractor that you want to make sure everything is included. If a first-rate contractor submits an exceptionally high bid, ask him or her to justify the price. It may be due to scheduling conflicts or to a feature you'd be happy to do without.

Most important, keep in mind that personality, references, reputation, quality of workmanship and schedule are key to a good collaboration, so be sure to take these considerations into account during the bidding process.

EXPERT TIP

Bond, Performance Bond

To protect yourself from contractors not fulfilling their agreement to the letter, you can purchase a performance bond. This extra measure of insurance means that if the contractor doesn't complete the agreed-upon project, the bond company will hire someone else to do the job.

Contracts

An integral part of any successful remodeling project is a detailed contract. And while writing one up may seem like a time-consuming formality, be sure you have one with each professional you hire before work begins. Not only will a contract protect you should problems arise, but it will also require you and the other parties to completely understand the project before getting started. No matter how much you trust the tradespeople you will be working with, avoid the temptation to skip this important step.

Though most professionals provide their own standard contracts, it is up to you, the homeowner, to make sure that it includes appropriate provisions for your specific project. You should feel free to suggest changes if you deem them necessary. You can start with a sample contract, but you'll need to modify it to reflect the requirements of your particular job. Show the contract to a lawyer to ensure that it offers the protection you need. At the very least, your contract should include the following points:

• A complete description of the work to be executed and the products to be purchased. Detail is essential: Include model numbers, colors and finishes for all products.

• An accounting of all payments, including a fee cap, subject to written change orders.

• A plan for how each party will handle unforeseen problems that arise over the course of the project, usually with an addendum to the contract that covers any additional payments that will be required from the homeowner to remedy the situation.

• A payment schedule.

• A work schedule with a completion date and stipulation of what will happen should this deadline not be met. The homeowner may also choose to include a "liquidated-damages provision," which states that for every day

▼ Once you've found exactly what you want for your bathroom—from the fixtures right down to the wall color—make sure it is all detailed in your contract.

work continues beyond the set deadline, the contractor will pay the homeowner a specific amount.

• A dispute-resolution clause. To avoid litigation, a contractor will often call for mediation by a third party or arbitration by a panel if a dispute cannot be settled.

• Specific details of the conditions under which either party can legally terminate the contract.

• A clause stating that only new materials may be used and that the homeowner must agree to all substitutions before they are made.

• A rider stipulating that all changes, whether or not they incur additional expenses, be submitted and approved in writing.

• Hours during which workers may have access to the site.

• A statement noting that the contractor is responsible for obtaining any and all necessary permits before construction begins.

• A provision for disposal of debris and materials and an explanation of who is responsible for cleaning up the work site.

• Proof of the contractor's certification of insurance for workers' compensation, property damage and liability.

• A section on how liens, waivers and warranties will be approached.

▲ This mirrored vanity with matching mirror has an old Hollywood look that will make you feel like a star.

▲ Ample storage was a top priority for the owner of this bath. Make a list of your "must-haves" for your bid requests.

For Your Protection

Insurance is probably the last thing you're thinking about as you start your building or remodeling project, but it should be the first. Before you go any further in planning or actual work, make sure you're adequately insured or your project could turn out to be very expensive, indeed.

Danger is rife at any construction site, from personal injury to structural damages, so it's essential to arm yourself with construction insurance before work begins. In fact, your local building department may require proof of coverage before issuing permits, and the lender will demand that its investment be protected—including life insurance to pay off the construction loan if the owner dies.

The type of construction insurance you'll need depends on whether you're contracting the job yourself or hiring a general contractor. If you're acting as your own general contractor, you must provide workers' compensation and disability to subcontractors and laborers. You'll also need a "builder's risk" policy to protect the structure and materials against weather, fire and theft; builder's risk is replaced with a homeowner's policy when construction is completed.

Finally, you'll need general liability in case of injury to a non-employee; this policy may be an extension of your current home's liability coverage. If you're hiring a general contractor, he or she must provide you with proof of current policies for builder's risk, workers' compensation and disability and business liability. You, as the homeowner, remain responsible for general liability.

◀ If you like the look of tile but can't afford to cover all of the walls, limit tile use to the shower/bath enclosure.

budgeting
& finance

▲ Selecting scaled-down fixtures will save space in the bathroom—and might also help you save money.

At the end of the day, the biggest obstacle to building your new bath will probably be the cost. According to the National Kitchen & Bath Association (NKBA), the average cost of a bath remodel is between $6,500 and $9,000, with installation accounting for nearly one-quarter of the expense. Of course, a number of project-specific factors figure into the total price. For example, the cost of labor and materials varies from one area of the country to another. The size of the room also affects the size of the bill. And you might be surprised at how great the range of prices is in terms of the type and quality of materials and components available.

Creating a Budget

Although we may have grand expectations, the bottom line may guide the project. So before you buy that free-standing soaking tub, know what you can afford and how you want to spend your money. Before you start planning, really examine your finances. Here are two calculations to consider:

Assets vs. Liabilities. First, make a list of your assets. The list should include cash on hand, savings accounts, equities, real estate and your employee savings plans (401K or other plans). Then look at your liabilities—any loans, credit card balances or other debt. Subtract your liabilities from your total assets. This is your net worth. Subtract an "emergency fund" amount—usually about six months' income—from your net worth. The remainder is the amount of money that you can use for a renovation.

Income vs. Expenses. Figure out how much you make per year—include your gross salary plus any additional funds like dividends and tax refunds. Then note your expenses, such as rent or mortgage payments, food, clothing, transportation, insurance premiums, utilities, savings, loans or charge-account payments, taxes, recreation and medical expenses. Subtract your current annual expenses from your current annual income; this is what you can spend per year on your renovation. If you plan to take out a loan, divide this amount by 12 to show what you can afford for monthly payments.

Consider both amounts carefully and come up with a number with which you feel comfortable. When you talk with contractors and designers, set your budget under the amount you can really afford (about 20 percent is recommended for the "slush fund"). This will cover any unexpected costs.

No matter what size your project or budget, there is a financing solution to meet your needs if you choose that route. And often, the tax advantages can help ease the burden.

▼ This beadboard enclosure for the tub is a "splurge" that creates a focal point in the room.

Construction Loan

A short-term loan from a bank or other lending institution, a construction loan is paid to your builder in increments, or "draws," at specific points in the building process. During the 6- to 12-month term of the loan, the homeowner makes interest-only payments on the amount advanced to date. As soon as the project is completed, the loan comes due. It is then paid off and replaced by a regular long-term mortgage. In the past, securing these loans required two different transactions, but today, many lenders are offering the two as a package deal, with the construction loan automatically being paid by the long-term mortgage. If you decide to go with one of these loans, called "construction-to-permanent," or "construction-perms," you'll only have to deal with one lending institution and go through one approval process and closing. You'll also only pay application and closing fees once.

Home Equity Loan

This type of loan employs the equity you have accrued in your house for collateral, providing a significant loan amount for a reasonable interest charge, which is usually tax deductible on the first $100,000 of loan principle. There are two basic options for equity financing: a lump-sum second mortgage at a fixed interest rate or a revolving line of credit with an adjustable rate, usually set 1 to 2.5 points above the prime rate and moving in lock step with it. The equity credit line with a variable interest rate allows you to draw money and repay it as you need to. For both types of financing, the maximum loan amount is 70 to 80 percent of the value of the house, minus the outstanding mortgage. When you compare home-equity loans, consider rates, the length of the loan and any up-front or ongoing fees. And keep in mind that this popular type of financing puts your house at risk if you are unable to repay the loan.

Refinancing

If interest rates have dropped since you took out your primary mortgage, refinancing will lower your monthly payment. However, you might also decide to take out a large mortgage, to reflect the appreciated value of the home, and "cash out" the difference to pay for any home improvements. On the upside, refinancing provides remodeling funds at low interest rates, while the long term of the loan—up to 30 years—keeps the monthly payments down. But remember to weigh the high up-front costs for the application, appraisals, title insurance and, in some cases, points, in your decision.

Personal Loans

If you lack home equity or prefer a fast, less paper-intensive loan for a small project, a personal loan might work for you. With good credit and sufficient income, you can often receive an unsecured loan for $5,000 to $25,000. However, personal loans come with higher, nondeductible interest charges and a short repayment period. If you can offer some form of collateral—property or a savings account—you may be able to reduce the interest rate a bit. To qualify for a personal loan, you will need to supply the bank with detailed plans for a professionally executed project. The lending institution then pays the contractor in draws throughout the construction process.

Margin Loans

These particular loans are arranged by your broker against the value of your stock portfolio. Note that if your portfolio value drops drastically, you may need to put more money into your account to keep the loan.

▲ A bathroom full of high-end tile can push your budget way over the line. An easy, attractive alternative is to choose a few special tiles to feature in a field of off-white.

photography credits

Wallcovering; **101** *(top left)* Courtesy of Seabrook, *(top right)* Courtesy of Eisenhart, *(bottom right)* Courtesy of Gramercy; **102** Courtesy of Dutch Boy; **103** *(top right)* Courtesy of Benjamin Moore, *(bottom right & bottom left)* Courtesy of Armstrong; **104** *(top right)* Courtesy of Ann Sacks Tile & Stone, *(bottom left)* Courtesy of Bisazza; **105** Courtesy of Walker Zanger; **106** Courtesy of American Olean; **107** *(top right)* Courtesy of Walker Zanger, *(bottom right)* Courtesy of Seneca; **108** *(top)* Courtesy of Congoleum; **109** *(left)* Courtesy of Congoleum, *(top right)* Courtesy of Armstrong, *(bottom right)* Courtesy of Mannington; **110** Courtesy of Kraftmaid Cabinetry; **111** *(both)* Courtesy of Formica Flooring; **112** Courtesy of Crossville Ceramics; **113** Courtesy of Florida Tile; **114** Courtesy of Eliane; **115** *(left)* Courtesy of Armstrong, *(top right)* Courtesy of Walker Zanger, *(bottom right)* Courtesy of Ann Sacks Tile & Stone, *(bottom center)* Courtesy of Bisazza; **116** Courtesy of Porcher; **117** Courtesy of KWC Faucets; **118** Courtesy of Toto USA; **119** *(left)* Courtesy of Elkay, *(top right)* Courtesy of Kohler Co., *(bottom right)* Courtesy of Boffi; **120** *(top right)* Courtesy of American Standard, *(bottom)* Courtesy of Geberit; **121** *(top right)* Courtesy of Ann Sacks Tile & Stone, *(bottom right)* Courtesy of Kohler Co., *(left)* Courtesy of St. Thomas; **122** Courtesy of Toto USA; **123** *(left)* Courtesy of Bis Bis Imports, *(top right)* Courtesy of Toto USA, *(bottom right)* Courtesy of Porcher; **124** *(top left & bottom left)* Courtesy of Kohler Co., *(top right)* Courtesy of Duravit, *(bottom center)* Courtesy of Kallista; **125** Courtesy of Waterworks; **126** *(top)* Courtesy of Linkasink, *(bottom right)* Courtesy of Transolid; **127** *(top left)* Courtesy of Porcher, *(top right)* Courtesy of Robern, *(bottom right)* Courtesy of Alchemy, *(bottom left)* Courtesy of Ann Sacks Tile & Stone; **128** Courtesy of Moen, Incorporated; **129** *(left)* Courtesy of Porcher, *(top right)* Courtesy of Kohler Co., *(bottom right)* Courtesy of Dornbracht USA; **130** Courtesy of Dornbracht USA; **131** *(top right)* Courtesy of Ann Sacks Tile & Stone, *(bottom right)* Courtesy of Delta Faucet Company, *(bottom left)* Courtesy of American Standard; **132** Courtesy of Delta Faucet Company; **133** *(top right)* Courtesy of Price Pfister, *(bottom right)* Courtesy of Delta Faucet Company, *(bottom left)* Courtesy of Moen, Incorporated; **134** Courtesy of Jacuzzi; **135** *(left)* Courtesy of Watermark, *(top right)* Courtesy of Delta Faucet Company, *(bottom right)* Courtesy of Moen, Incorporated; **136** Courtesy of Waterworks; **137** *(top right)* Courtesy of Price Pfister, *(bottom right)* Courtesy of Delta Faucet Company, *(bottom left)* Courtesy of Ultra Baths; **138** *(bottom left)* Courtesy of Moen, Incorporated, *(bottom right)* Courtesy of Dornbracht USA; **139** Courtesy of Jacuzzi; **140** *(top left)* Courtesy of Style-Mark, *(top center)* Courtesy of American Standard, *(bottom)* Courtesy of Hansgrohe-USA; **141** *(left)* Courtesy of Duravit, *(top right)* Courtesy of Grohe North America, *(bottom right)* Courtesy of Coastal Industries; **142** Courtesy of Kohler Co.; **143** *(top left)* Courtesy of Grohe North America, *(top right)* Courtesy of Coastal Industries, *(bottom right)* Courtesy of Dornbracht USA, *(bottom center)* Courtesy of Swanstone; **144** Courtesy of Waterworks; **145** *(left)* Courtesy of Boffi, *(top right)* Courtesy of Kohler Co., *(bottom right)* Courtesy of Restoration Hardware; **146** Courtesy of Jacuzzi; **147** *(top right)* Courtesy of Moen, Incorporated, *(bottom right)* Courtesy of St. Thomas, *(bottom left)* Courtesy of Kallista; **148** Courtesy of Cielo; **149** *(top left)* Courtesy of Ann Sacks Tile & Stone, *(top right & bottom right)* Courtesy of Jacuzzi; **150** *(top left)* Courtesy of Jacuzzi, *(top right)* Courtesy of NeoMetro; **151** *(top center)* Courtesy of American Standard, *(top right)* Courtesy of Kallista, *(bottom right)* Courtesy of Toto USA; **152** *(top right)* Courtesy of Toto USA, *(bottom left)* Courtesy of Kohler Co.; **153** *(top right)* Courtesy of American Standard, *(bottom right)* Courtesy of Kohler Co., *(bottom center)* Courtesy of The Throne Room, *(bottom left)* Courtesy of Acorn Engineering; **154** Courtesy of Marvin Windows and Doors; **155** Courtesy of Ann Sacks Tile & Stone; **156** Courtesy of Andersen Windows and Doors; **157** *(top right)* Courtesy of Vetter Windows & Doors, *(bottom right)* Courtesy of Hy-Lite; **158** *(bottom left)* Courtesy of Kolbe & Kolbe, *(bottom right)* Courtesy of Pella Windows and Doors; **159** *(top right)* Courtesy of Pella Windows and Doors, *(bottom right)* Courtesy of Andersen Windows and Doors; **160** Courtesy of Weather Shield Windows & Doors; **161** *(top right)* Courtesy of Marvin Windows and Doors, *(bottom right)* Courtesy of Summit; **162** Sam Gray; **163** *(left)* Courtesy of Weather Shield Windows & Doors, *(top right)* Courtesy of Restoration Hardware, *(bottom right)* Courtesy of Kallista; **164** *(top left)* Courtesy of Rejuvenation Lamp and Fixture, *(bottom left)* Courtesy of Kallista, *(bottom center)* Courtesy of Valli & Valli, *(bottom right)* Courtesy of Robern; **165** Courtesy of Brass Light Gallery; **166** Mark Samu; **168** Courtesy of American Olean; **169** Courtesy of Waterworks; **170** Courtesy of Progress Lighting; **171** *(top right & bottom right)* Mark Samu, *(bottom center)* Courtesy of Alchemy; **172** Courtesy of DuPont; **173** Mark Samu; **174** Courtesy of American Standard; **175** *(top right & bottom right)* Sam Gray, *(bottom center)* Courtesy of American Standard; **176** Courtesy of Armstrong; **177** *(left)* Courtesy of Swanstone, *(top right)* Courtesy of Decora, *(bottom right)* Courtesy of Hunter Douglas; **178** *(bottom left)* Courtesy of Waverly, *(bottom right)* Sam Gray; **179** *(top left)* Courtesy of Delta Faucet Company, *(bottom right)* Courtesy of Diamond Spas, *(bottom left)* Courtesy of Aristokraft; **180** *(top left)* James Yochum, *(top right)* Courtesy of Rohl; **181** *(both)* Jeffrey Green; **182** Courtesy of Wellborn; **183** *(bottom left)* Courtesy of Kallista, *(bottom center)* Jeffrey Green; **184** Mark Lohman; **185** Courtesy of Waterworks; **186** Mark Samu; **187** Courtesy of Crossville Ceramics.

index

A

accessibility, 28–31
aluminum
    window frames, 160
American Architectural
Manufacturers Association, 157
American Institute of Architects
(AIA), 171
American Society of Interior
Designers (ASID), 171
AquaSuite PureTouch faucet, 133
architects, 171, 172–174

B

basins. see sinks
beadboard, 47, 74, 177, 186
bidets, 16–17, 153
bids, 180–181
Body Spa system, 11
budgeting, 12, 15, 24, 185–187

C

cabinets, 81–89
    see also medicine cabinets
    see also vanities
    contemporary style, 32, 53
    design trends, 82–84
    freestanding, 34, 35, 37, 38, 77
    furniture look, 81
    semicustom, 49, 87, 88
ceramic
    sinks, 53, 123
    tiles, 13, 106, 112, 114, 169
certified bath designer (CBD), 170–171
change orders, 178
charming style, 21, 44–49
children's bathroom, 17
colors
    effects, 21, 22, 45, 47, 49, 54,
    72, 107

paint selection, 102–103
palette selection, 26–27
    and style, 43, 60, 62, 65, 68
concrete, 11, 17, 66, 91, 96, 97
conservation, 32–33
construction loans, 186
contemporary style, 32, 50–53, 164
contractors, 171, 175, 176–179
contracts, 178, 180–183
Corian, 145
countertops, 92–97
    concrete, 17, 96, 97
    cleaning, 97
    glass, 127
    granite, 58, 97
    laminate, 16, 96, 97
    limestone, 71, 97
    marble, 51, 54, 54, 77, 94, 95, 97
    soapstone, 61, 97
    solid surfacing, 16, 92–93, 97
    stone, 83, 94

D

design, preliminary, 22–23, 25, 175
door knobs, 88–89
drawer pulls, 23, 88–89

E

elegant style, 54–59, 85
energy efficiency, 32–33, 161
entertainment, 33, 71, 149

F

fans, 164
faucets, 128–133
    contemporary, 53
    finishes, 25, 55, 58, 61, 97, 117, 137
    placement of, 14
    single-handle, 30, 31, 129, 131
    tub fillers, 12, 67, 75, 169

vintage look, 77
filtered water, 133
financing, 185–187
fixtures. see faucets; showers; sinks;
toilets; tubs
fixture templates, 23
flooring, 108–115
    crocodile print, 115
    laminate, 111–112
    marble, 115, 180
    slate, 68
    tile, 27, 112–115
    vinyl, 108–111, 115
    wood, 19, 57, 58, 143

G

general contractors, 171, 175, 176–179
glass
    see also windows
    blocks, 24, 67
    countertops, 127
    lacquered, 97, 123
    shelves, 47, 65
    sinks, 120, 127, 171
    tiles, 77, 104, 106, 115
grab bars, 29, 30
granite, 58, 94, 95, 97
grouts, 107, 114

H

handshowers, 29, 136, 138, 143, 147, 169
home equity loans, 186–187

I

insurance, 169, 181, 183
interior designers, 170–171

J

Jasmin washlet seat, 151

K

knobs, 88–89

L

laminates, 96, 97, 111–112
lavatories. see sinks
light, natural, 49, 71, 155, 156–161
    see also windows
lighting, artificial, 30, 48, 57, 75, 154–165
limestone, 57, 71, 94, 97
linoleum, 111
loans, 186–187
low-E window coating, 161
Lucite acrylic shower system, 137

M

marble
    countertops, 51, 54, 54, 77,
    94, 95, 97
    flooring, 115, 180
materials, mixing, 72
medicine cabinets, 34, 37, 49, 51, 164
mildew, 103
mirrors, 21, 43, 48, 51, 71, 75, 134
moldings, 47, 49, 58, 81, 87, 98, 140
muntins, 47, 161
music, 33, 71

N

National Association of the
Remodeling Industry (NARI), 171
National Fenestration Rating
Council, 157
National Kitchen & Bath
Association (NKBA), 25, 171

P

paint, 102–103
    faux finishes, 103
patterns, 72, 100–101

performance bonds, 181
professionals, working with
    architects, 171, 172–175
    bids and contracts, 178, 180–183
    contractors, 171, 175, 176–179
    interior designers, 170–171
project phases, 175
project planning, 11–27

Q

Q-Bits, 38
quartz surfaces, 53, 92, 95, 96

R

Residential Fenestration
Performance Analysis Tool, 157
rustic style, 60–61

S

safety, 14, 28–31
SanaGloss, 118
sheet surfacing, 108, 111
shelves, 35, 47, 65, 85, 179
shower curtains, 38
shower doors, 28, 140
shower enclosures, 14, 47, 62, 137, 141, 185
showerheads, 23, 30, 72, 134–138, 141, 143
showers, 11, 33, 67, 72, 134–143, 175
shower seats, 75, 143
shower/tub combinations, 20, 140, 185
simple style, 62–65
sinks, 118–127
    above-counter, 21, 27, 83, 117, 121, 123, 129, 131
    ceramic, 53, 123
    and countertop units, 31, 96–97, 177
    glass, 97, 120, 123, 127, 171
    his-and-her, 17

Jelly-Cube, 124
    pedestal, 17, 65, 120, 124, 127
    self-rimming, 118, 123
    solid surfacing, 27, 118
    stainless steel, 61, 71, 119
    vessel, 32, 118–120
    vintage, 58
slate, 68, 94
soapstone, 61, 94, 97
solid surfacing, 92–93, 97
    countertops, 16, 92–93, 97
    sinks, 27, 118
space creation, 18–21
space requirements, 14, 16–17, 25, 30–31, 144
spa style, 11, 33, 66–73, 82, 136–143
Starck, Philippe, 124
steam baths, 138, 141
stone, 83, 77, 91, 94, 111, 112, 114, 179
storage, 25, 34–39, 61, 87, 176, 183
styles
    about, 13, 43–45
    charming, 21, 44–49
    contemporary, 32, 50–53, 164
    elegant, 54–59, 85
    rustic, 60–61
    simple, 62–65
    spa, 11, 33, 66–73, 82, 136–143
    vintage, 12, 74–77, 85, 178
surfacing, 90–115
Syndecrete, 97

T

templates for planning, 23
textured stone, 112, 114
textures, 43, 72, 91, 101
tile
    as accents, 44, 115, 140
    ceramic, 13, 106, 112, 114, 169
    flooring, 27, 112–115

glass, 77, 104, 106, 115

leather, 104

mosaic, 27, 32, 68, 77, 104, 114, 115

stone, 112, 114, 179

subway, 107

terra-cotta, 62

vinyl no-wax, 109

walls, 104–106

toilet compartments, 18, 67

toilets, 16–17, 31–32, 58, 150–153

towel racks, 120, 144

heated, 33, 72, 143

transfer seats, 29

trompe l'oeil panels, 101

tub caddy, 62

tub fillers, 12, 67, 75, 169

tubs, 144–149

cast-iron, 146

claw-foot, 74

freestanding, 19

platform, 38, 176

soaking, 12, 18, 57, 66, 68, 71, 144–145, 147, 149

whirlpool, 32–33, 67, 115, 146–149, 174

tub surrounds, 11, 16, 38, 47, 61, 68, 176, 177

U

universal design, 28–31

urethane moldings, 58, 140

V

vanities, 17, 19, 35, 54, 55, 57, 81, 83, 85, 86, 87, 88, 93, 124, 183

double, or his-and-her, 23, 75

vintage style, 12, 74–77, 85, 178

vinyl

flooring, 108–111, 115

window frames, 160

W

wainscoting, 58, 75

wallpaper, 26, 98–101

water conservation, 32

wheelchair accessibility, 28–31

window coverings, 44, 57, 58, 159

windows, 155–161

bay, 158

box, 158

casement, 74, 157, 158, 159

double-hung, 156, 160, 162

fixed, 155, 158, 161

frame materials, 158–161

lead-glass, 174

pocket, 66

sandblasted, 181

window seats, 57

wood

flooring, 19, 57, 58, 143

window frames, 159–160

Z

Zoë toilets, remote-controlled, 17

zones, 12